Rooted

A Fresh Look at Colossians

James J. Burke

Fireproof Commentaries

Volume IV

FIREPROOF
COMMENTARIES

ISBN-13: —979-8-9941637-6-4

All Scripture quotations are taken from the King
James Version of the Bible unless otherwise
indicated.

Printed in the United States of America
fireproofcommentaries.org

This volume is dedicated to the kind and loving congregations who have, by listening intently and asking good questions, helped shape my teaching and understanding.

Table of Contents

Foreword

The letter to the Colossians was written to ordinary believers living in an ordinary city, facing ordinary pressures—and yet Paul addresses them with some of the highest Christology in all of Scripture. That contrast is not accidental. When the church feels most vulnerable, Christ must be seen most clearly.

Colossae was not a center of power or prestige. It sat in the shadow of larger cities and more influential voices. The believers there were not rejecting Christ outright; they were being told, subtly and persistently, that Christ was not enough. They were urged to supplement Him—to add spiritual experiences, religious observances, or philosophical insight that promised fullness beyond the gospel. Paul's response was not to offer balance or compromise, but clarity. He wrote to remind them that everything God intends to give His people is already found in His Son.

That same pressure remains today. Modern believers are rarely asked to abandon Christ altogether. More often, we are encouraged to treat Him as foundational but insufficient—useful, but incomplete. We are tempted to look elsewhere for meaning, stability, wisdom, or power, assuming that maturity lies in reaching beyond Christ rather than growing deeper into Him. The result is often a restless faith: busy, informed, and sincere, yet quietly unsure whether Christ alone truly satisfies.

Rooted was written to address that uncertainty. It is not a technical commentary aimed at specialists, nor a devotional that avoids the weight of the text. It is a pastoral exposition meant to help believers see Colossians as Paul intended it to be read—not as a collection of isolated verses, but as a unified testimony to the supremacy and sufficiency of Jesus Christ.

Throughout this book, the controlling question is simple: What does it mean to live a life that is genuinely rooted in Christ? Paul answers that question by lifting our eyes upward to who Christ is, then pressing His lordship downward into every area of life—faith, worship, obedience, prayer, speech, relationships, and community. Christ is not presented as an accessory to Christian living, but as its source and substance.

The metaphor of rootedness is particularly fitting. Roots grow unseen. They deepen quietly. They do their work long before fruit appears. In the same way, spiritual maturity is not produced by novelty or speed, but by steady, hidden attachment to Christ. A tree survives storms not because of what is visible above ground, but because of what is firmly anchored below it.

This book follows the natural movement of Colossians itself. It begins with Christ exalted over all creation, moves through the dangers of false fullness, and then unfolds the practical implications of a Christ-centered life. Doctrine leads to devotion. Identity shapes conduct. Grace fuels obedience. The gospel does not remain theoretical; it takes form in daily faithfulness and shared life within the body of Christ.

If this book has a single aim, it is this: to help readers rest more fully in Christ and grow more deeply into Him. Not to chase spiritual advancement, but to recognize what they already possess. Not to reach upward in pride, but to press downward into grace.

Paul's message to the Colossians remains God's message to the church today:

> *"As ye have therefore received Christ Jesus the Lord, so walk ye in Him: rooted and built up in Him, and established in the faith."* Colossians 2:7

May that same exhortation guide every page that follows—and may it shape the lives of all who read them.

— James J. Burke

Marinette, Wisconsin

2025

Introduction — Christ, Our Root

The book of Colossians was written during Paul's first imprisonment in Rome, around the same time as his letter to the Ephesians. The two epistles are twin pillars of the same great truth— Ephesians exalts the Church in Christ, while Colossians exalts Christ in the Church. If Ephesians lifts our eyes to see the Church seated with Christ in heavenly places, Colossians bows our hearts to see Christ enthroned above all things. Together they reveal the mystery that the Church is complete only when rooted in the all-sufficient Christ.

Colossae was a small and fading city in the Lycus Valley of Asia Minor, overshadowed by its wealthier neighbors Laodicea and Hierapolis. Once a thriving trade center along the great Persian highway, its importance had waned by the time of Paul's writing. But the gospel, as it so often does, found fertile soil in the overlooked and forgotten. Even in this out-of-the-way place, the message of Christ took root and bore fruit.

The Church at Colossae was not founded by Paul himself but by a faithful disciple named Epaphras. During Paul's three-year ministry in Ephesus, the gospel had spread throughout Asia Minor, and it was there that Epaphras heard the Word, believed, and was trained. He then carried that message back home, preaching along the way in Laodicea and Hierapolis before planting the church in Colossae. Epaphras was not a famous preacher or a man of worldly stature. He was a laborer who simply could not keep the gospel to himself—a man who turned his journey home into a mission field. That is often how God multiplies His work: through ordinary believers who are faithful in ordinary moments.

In time, Epaphras traveled to Rome, where Paul was imprisoned. He brought both joy and concern—joy over the steadfastness of the believers in Colossae, and concern over subtle but dangerous teachings beginning to spread among them. These teachings sounded spiritual but were, in truth, a form of early Gnosticism—a worldview that would later blossom into one of the Church's greatest heresies.

The Seeds of Gnosticism

The word *gnosis* means "knowledge." The Gnostics claimed to possess a secret or higher knowledge of divine things, accessible only to those initiated into their mysteries. To them, the simple gospel preached by Paul was too unsophisticated. Faith in Christ alone was fine for the unlearned masses, but the "enlightened" could climb higher. They believed that true salvation came not through faith and grace but through mystical insight and the discovery of hidden truths.

The roots of this thinking reached deep into the soil of both Greek philosophy and Eastern mysticism. The people of the Lycus Valley were surrounded by cultural and religious crosscurrents—Hellenistic thought, Jewish legalism, Roman imperial cults, and various mystery religions that promised transcendence through ritual and secret knowledge. It was an environment perfectly suited for spiritual confusion.

Gnosticism in its mature form would not fully develop until the second century, but its early sprouts were already visible in Paul's day. In Colossae, the heresy seems to have taken a syncretistic form—a blending of Jewish tradition, Greek speculation, and local superstition. The Colossian error taught that the material world was evil, created not by the true God but by lesser spiritual beings called aeons. These emanations were thought to stand between God and creation, forming a kind of cosmic hierarchy that one must ascend through to reach divine fullness.

In such a system, Christ was reduced to merely one of many spiritual intermediaries—a high one, perhaps, but not the final revelation of God. To the Colossians who had once rejoiced in the sufficiency of Christ, this teaching whispered, "There's more. You've only begun. You must climb higher." And so faith began to blur into philosophy, and grace into speculation.

This heresy appealed to the intellect. It offered something the flesh loves: a sense of superiority. It allowed a person to claim enlightenment without repentance, depth without discipleship, and spirituality without submission. It promised heavenly secrets while quietly dethroning the One in whom all the treasures of wisdom and knowledge already dwell.

Why Colossae?

Colossae was especially vulnerable to this kind of teaching. Its population was diverse—a mix of Greeks, Jews, and Phrygians—and the region was known for its fascination with visions, angels, and mystical experiences. Archaeologists have uncovered inscriptions from the area invoking angels and spiritual powers for protection. Paul's warnings later in the letter—against "worship of angels" and being "puffed up by visions"—fit perfectly with the cultural climate of the city.

Add to this a lingering sense of civic decline. Once-proud Colossae was losing relevance; her citizens, like many in struggling places, may have sought new identities in spiritual novelty. When human hearts feel small or unseen, false teachers thrive. They offer secret doors and hidden stairways to transcendence. The Gnostics provided precisely that—a religion of layers, a system of steps, a promise of superiority. But in chasing it, believers were drifting from the simplicity of Christ.

It is telling that Paul answers all of this not with argument but with adoration. He does not begin by naming the heresy or refuting its logic point by point. Instead, he magnifies Christ so greatly that error shrinks to insignificance. He writes one of the most majestic Christological hymns in Scripture, proclaiming the Son as "the image of the invisible God, the firstborn of all creation." He reminds them that by Him and for Him all things were made, and in Him all things hold together. Paul's theology is not speculative—it is relational. His antidote to false wisdom is a living Christ.

The All-Sufficiency of Christ

Colossians declares that Jesus Christ is supreme in every realm. He is preeminent in creation—the One through whom all things were made. He is preeminent in the Church—the Head of the body and the source of its life. He is preeminent in redemption—the reconciler of all things through the blood of His cross. There is no fullness apart from Him, no higher revelation beyond Him, no spiritual reality outside of Him. To add anything to Christ is to subtract from His glory.

Paul's letter insists that believers are not missing anything. They already possess everything in Christ. "For in Him dwelleth all the fullness of the Godhead bodily, and ye are complete in Him." (Col. 2:9–10) The gospel does not need to be upgraded or expanded—it needs to be believed and lived. The Christian's calling is not to climb higher but to grow deeper. We are not to reach beyond Christ, but to become rooted in Him.

This is the message that gives Rooted its title. The Christian life is not about stretching upward in pride but pressing downward into grace. When the soul is rooted in Christ, it finds nourishment that no false teaching can supply. It is stabilized against the winds of cultural confusion and grounded in a hope that cannot be moved.

The Journey Ahead

This commentary, *Rooted: A Fresh Look at Colossians*, seeks to help believers grow deep in that same grace. It follows the Fireproof pattern—Exposition, Summary, Application, and Prayer—but its purpose is singular: to magnify the supremacy and sufficiency of Jesus Christ. Every verse of Colossians draws us back to Him. Every warning, every encouragement, every command springs from who He is.

As we journey through these chapters, may we, too, learn what it means to live "rooted and built up in Him, and established in the faith." May our roots sink deeply into His truth. May our lives bear the fruit of His Spirit. And may we stand firm in the same confession that has anchored believers for two thousand years:

Christ is enough.

> "As ye have therefore received Christ Jesus the Lord, so walk ye in Him:
>
> Rooted and built up in Him, and established in the faith."
>
> — Colossians 2:6–7

Rooted

1

The Supremacy of Christ

Colossians 1:1–29

The letter to the Colossians opens with thanksgiving and quickly rises to one of the highest peaks of Christology in all Scripture. Paul writes from prison in Rome to believers he has never met personally, a congregation planted by his friend and fellow servant, Epaphras. Though Paul's chains confined his body, his prayers and pastoral care extended far beyond the walls of his cell.

Epaphras had reported to Paul the faith and love of the believers in Colossae, as well as the subtle influences threatening their stability—teachings that blended Jewish legalism with Greek philosophy and mystical speculation. The danger was not that the

Colossians were rejecting Christ, but that they were being told Christ was not enough. Paul's letter answers that claim with thunderous clarity: **Christ is all.**

He begins with gratitude:

> *"We give thanks to God and the Father of our Lord Jesus Christ, praying always for you, since we heard of your faith in Christ Jesus, and of the love which ye have to all the saints, for the hope which is laid up for you in heaven."* (1:3–5a)

Faith, love, and hope—the three great virtues of the Christian life—form the foundation of Paul's thanksgiving. They are the same triad Paul exalts in 1 Corinthians 13:13: "And now abideth faith, hope, charity, these three; but the greatest of these is charity." These are not fleeting emotions but enduring graces that define the life of every believer who walks in Christ.

Faith (*pistis*) speaks of a settled trust—a conviction anchored so firmly in the person of Christ that it steadies the heart against every shifting current. It is not mere belief in certain facts, but a resting confidence that commits the whole self to the Savior. In Paul's theology, faith always carries the sense of faithfulness—trust that transforms into constancy of character. A man who truly believes God becomes trustworthy himself; his life takes on the stability of the One he trusts.

Love (*agapē*) is the outflow of that faith. This is not the affection of sentiment or the passion of impulse, but the divine quality of unselfish care—the kind of love that seeks another's good regardless of personal cost. It is the love that moved the Father to send His Son, the love that led Christ to the cross, the love that cannot be extinguished by offense or cooled by neglect. Jesus declared that such love is the distinguishing mark of His disciples: "By this shall all men know that ye are My disciples, if ye have love one to another." (John 13:35)

Hope (*elpis*) completes the triad. It is not wishful thinking but a settled expectation—a goal already established by the promises of God that draws the believer forward. Faith anchors the soul in the present; hope draws it toward the future. Faith rests in what Christ has done; hope reaches toward what He will do. This hope, Paul says, is "laid up for you in heaven"—secure, untouchable, and guaranteed by the resurrection of Christ Himself.

Thus, faith reaches upward in trust, love reaches outward in service, and hope reaches forward in expectation. These three are woven together like strands of a single cord: faith lays hold of Christ, love displays Christ, and hope awaits Christ. Together they form the living root system of the Christian life—the unseen strength that keeps the believer steadfast, fruitful, and unmovable in a changing world.

Paul reminds them that this hope came through "the word of the truth of the gospel," which is bearing fruit and increasing throughout the world. The gospel, he says, was producing change among them "from the day ye heard it, and knew the grace of God in truth." The work of God's grace had begun before they fully understood it. The seed of the gospel was planted, watered by the Spirit, and bore fruit long before they could comprehend its fullness.

That truth should encourage every evangelist and every praying parent. God's Word does not return void. The seed planted in the heart may lie unseen, but it lives. Our task is to sow faithfully and trust God for the harvest.

Paul speaks tenderly of Epaphras, calling him "our dear fellow servant, who is for you a faithful minister of Christ." The great apostle does not elevate himself above his co-laborer but calls him a fellow slave. The ministry is not a ladder to climb but a field to plow, and all who labor in it are fellow servants of the same Master.

Knowledge, Understanding and Wisdom

Having rejoiced in their faith, Paul now prays for their growth:

"That ye might be filled with the knowledge of His will in all wisdom and spiritual understanding; that ye might walk worthy of the Lord unto all pleasing, being fruitful in every good work, and increasing in the knowledge of God." (1:9–10)

Paul's prayer for the Colossians turns from thanksgiving to intercession. He prays "that ye might be filled with the knowledge of His will in all wisdom and spiritual understanding." (Colossians 1:9) These three qualities—knowledge, understanding, and wisdom—are distinct yet inseparable.

Before we define them, consider an example from history. Did you know that the steam engine was invented about a hundred years before the birth of Christ? A shoemaker in Alexandria, Egypt, named Heron (or Hero) of Alexandria, noticed that when water boiled, the steam carried power. He built a hollow metal sphere, fitted nozzles at opposite ends, filled it with water, and set it over a fire. As the water boiled, the escaping steam made the ball spin on its axle. He called it the wind machine—and proudly demonstrated it at banquets as a novelty.

Heron possessed remarkable knowledge and even understanding, but what he lacked was wisdom. He knew that steam contained energy, and he understood how to harness that energy into motion—but it would take nearly two thousand years before anyone had the wisdom to apply that principle practically to move engines, trains, and ships. His discovery had immense potential, but no power was released until someone applied it.

Paul's prayer works in exactly the same way.

Epignōsis
Full, accurate, and lived-out knowledge, not merely the possession of information. It describes truth that has been rightly grasped and allowed to shape understanding, conviction, and obedience.

Knowledge (*epignōsis*) is the gathering of truth—the data of God's revelation. It is the simple possession of information. In our day, it is easy to be filled with knowledge of God's will; Scripture is more accessible than ever before. Yet knowledge alone is cheap and often inert. Many believers can quote verses, recall Bible facts, and win "Bible Trivia" contests, yet their hearts remain unchanged. Paul never prayed that the church would be full of facts; he prayed that they would be full of functional truth.

Understanding (*synesis*) is the ability to see how those truths interconnect and harmonize—to fit the pieces together into a living pattern. Just as Heron looked at fire, water, and steam and realized their relationship, the believer is called to perceive how God's truths form a unified revelation of His will. Scripture is not a collection of disconnected stories and sayings; it is a single, divinely woven narrative that centers on Christ. Understanding enables us to see the pattern of redemption that runs from Genesis to Revelation—the scarlet thread that ties every promise to the cross.

But wisdom (*sophia*) goes further. Wisdom is the application of that understanding in daily life—the ability to take what we know and make it work. The world pictures wisdom as a gray-bearded sage pondering clouds on a mountaintop. In truth, wisdom is intensely practical. It is truth in motion, knowledge with a purpose. Heron knew how to make steam spin a toy; wisdom would later make steam move nations. Likewise, we often stop short at theological curiosity. We analyze Scripture, categorize doctrines, and map the prophetic timeline—but unless those truths transform our character and conduct, they remain unspent potential.

God's Word is powerful, but it is wasted when it lies unused. It is not enough to know that *Christ died for us*; wisdom asks, *What does that mean for how I live?*

It is not enough to affirm that He is Lord; wisdom demands that we live as His servants. Paul prays that believers would possess all three—knowledge, understanding, and wisdom—so that their lives might "walk worthy of the Lord unto all pleasing" (v. 10). In other words, that their faith would be both informed and embodied, rooted in truth and ripened in obedience.

Strengthened with All Might

He then prays that they would be "strengthened with all might, according to His glorious power, unto all patience and longsuffering with joyfulness." (Colossians 1:11) The words are heavy with meaning. Paul does not pray that the Colossians would grow powerful in the worldly sense—he prays that they would be strengthened with power, according to power, and for endurance. This is not natural grit but divine enabling.

The phrase "according to His glorious power" points to the source. The strength Paul has in mind is not drawn from human willpower or emotional resilience, but from the very glory of God—the same strength that spoke creation into existence, that upheld Christ on the cross, and that raised Him from the dead. That is the measure of the power available to the believer. But notice how that power is to be used: unto all patience and longsuffering with joyfulness.

The world measures power by its display—by how much it can dominate, control, or impress. God measures power by its endurance—by how long it can trust, obey, and rejoice under pressure. The miracles of grace are often quiet ones: the parent who prays through tears for a prodigal child, the believer who forgives the unrepentant, the servant who keeps laboring unseen. The greatest demonstration of divine power is not found in spectacular deliverances but in steadfast hearts that refuse to break under the weight of trial.

In Paul's own life, the power of God was never more visible than in his weakness. "My grace is sufficient for thee," the Lord told him, "for My strength is made perfect in weakness." (2 Corinthians 12:9) The apostle who once moved mountains by prayer later gloried in his thorn, because it made him lean harder on Christ. The lesson is the same for us: God does not always remove the pressure; He gives power to bear it. He does not promise escape from the fire; He promises His presence in it.

The two words Paul uses—patience (*hypomonē*) and longsuffering (*makrothymia*)—carry distinct shades of endurance. Patience refers to steadfastness under difficult circumstances; longsuffering refers to steadfastness toward difficult people. One is endurance in trial; the other is endurance in relationship. Both require divine strength. The flesh can grit its teeth and tolerate hardship for a while, but only the Spirit can enable a believer to endure with joyfulness. Joy is the proof that God's strength is at work.

When Paul says "with joyfulness," he adds the crown to the whole request. It is one thing to bear the load; it is another to sing under it. Anyone can endure with bitterness; only the Spirit can make endurance beautiful. Joy is not denial of pain but delight in God's faithfulness. It is the quiet song that rises when the heart remembers that trials are temporary, but Christ is eternal.

So Paul's prayer unfolds like this: that believers would be fortified by divine strength, measured not by outward display but by inward stability; that they would persevere in circumstances that test them and show grace to people who wound them; and that, in all of it, their endurance would be laced with joy. True spiritual power is not the ability to change our surroundings—it is the ability to remain steadfast when everything around us trembles, and to do so with thanksgiving on our lips.

The Present and Future Inheritance

"Giving thanks unto the Father, which hath made us meet to be partakers of the inheritance of the saints in light." (1:12)

This inheritance is not only future but present. It is both a promise and a portion. We share in the light of Christ even while living in a dark world. The Father has not only reserved our inheritance in heaven; He has also qualified us for it now. The phrase "hath made us meet" means He has rendered us fit—made us worthy—not by our merit, but by the righteousness of His Son. The inheritance of the saints is not earned through service but received through sonship. Yet that sonship compels us to serve.

Like the faithful son in the parable of the Prodigal, our inheritance today means laboring in the Father's fields. The younger son wasted his inheritance in riotous living, and the elder son resented his inheritance as toil. But the true heir rejoices to work in his Father's domain, knowing that everything he tends already belongs to him. The believer's present inheritance is this: to live and labor in the light—to handle holy things, to bear the name of the Father, and to reflect His nature in a world still shrouded by darkness.

Paul writes that we have been "delivered from the power of darkness, and translated into the kingdom of

His dear Son." The verb *translated* is vivid; it was used in ancient times to describe the relocation of an entire people from one realm to another. We have been uprooted from the dominion of darkness and resettled under the gracious reign of the Son. Yet this new citizenship is not merely positional—it is transformational. We are no longer slaves working for wages in a foreign land; we are sons working for love in our Father's kingdom.

The inheritance of the saints is therefore both eternal and experiential. It is eternal in that it awaits us in glory—imperishable, undefiled, and unfading. It is experiential in that it already begins within us. We taste the firstfruits of heaven whenever we walk in obedience, experience forgiveness, or reflect the light of Christ. The Holy Spirit is the down payment of that inheritance (Ephesians 1:13–14), the pledge that guarantees the full possession to come. The more we yield to His sanctifying work, the more we live as citizens of the coming kingdom while still standing on enemy soil.

This truth reshapes how we view our labor. We do not serve God in order to gain an inheritance; we serve because we already have one. Every act of obedience, every sacrifice made for His name, every quiet work of faithfulness is not a payment toward heaven but a participation in it. We are ambassadors of light, representing the rule of a King who has not yet returned to take His throne. Our lives are embassies of His grace. The workplace, the home, the church—all are mission fields within our Father's estate.

And this inheritance, though shared among the saints, loses nothing in the sharing. In earthly economies, inheritance divides the estate; in God's economy, it multiplies it. Every believer receives the fullness of Christ without diminishing the portion of another. The light we reflect does not lessen another's glow—it makes the world brighter. When Paul says the Father has "made us partakers," he uses the language of fellowship. The inheritance of the saints is a shared life in Christ's light, not a private treasure hoarded away.

Therefore, we give thanks—not only for what awaits us in eternity, but for what we already possess in the present hour. The Father has qualified us, delivered us, and translated us. We live between two worlds: citizens of heaven walking the soil of earth, heirs of eternity serving among those still in bondage. Every day we live in that tension, yet every day we carry the light of our inheritance into the shadows of this world.

The more we understand this, the more joyfully we labor. To the weary servant, this truth brings rest: your work is not wasted, for you are tending your Father's field. To the discouraged believer, it brings hope: the darkness is temporary, for you already belong to the light. To the faithful saint, it brings thanksgiving: the inheritance has already begun. We do not await it from afar—it has begun in the heart of every child of God who walks in His light.

The Christ Hymn

From this foundation, Paul moves into one of the most exalted declarations of Christ's deity in the entire New Testament:

> *"Who is the image of the invisible God, the firstborn of every creature: for by Him were all things created... and by Him all things consist."* *(1:15)*

Christ is the image of the invisible God—the visible expression of the invisible Creator. When Philip said, "Show us the Father," Jesus answered, "He that hath seen Me hath seen the Father." No one has ever seen God in His essence, but Christ makes Him known.

To call Jesus "the firstborn of all creation" does not mean He was created, but that He holds the place of preeminence and authority. In the ancient world, the firstborn son represented the father and inherited his authority. Thus, Christ is not the first creature, but the divine agent of all creation. The Father planned creation, the Son performed it, and the Spirit empowered it.

*"All things were created by Him and for Him...
and by Him all things consist."*

Every atom, every galaxy, every breath exists by His will and for His glory. He is before all things, and He holds all things together. Even as a baby lying in a manger, He was sustaining the universe by His power.

He is also "the head of the body, the church." As the source and sustainer of creation, He is likewise the source and sustainer of redemption. He is "the beginning, the firstborn from the dead," the pioneer of resurrection life. Through His cross, He reconciles all things to Himself—things in heaven and things on earth—making peace through His blood.

Paul's words overturn every heresy that would diminish Christ. He is not one among many spiritual beings but the eternal Son in whom "all the fullness of God was pleased to dwell." There is no higher revelation beyond Him, no deeper mystery apart from Him, and no salvation without Him.

Summary

Paul's first chapter is both a song and a sword. It exalts Christ and cuts down every false philosophy that would dethrone Him. The Colossians were tempted to seek spiritual fullness elsewhere—to mix law with grace, reason with revelation, and mysticism with faith. Paul answers by pointing to Jesus: He is the fullness.

Christ is supreme in creation, the Church, and redemption. He is the Creator who formed all things, the Sustainer who holds all things together, and the Redeemer who reconciles all things by His blood. To know Him is to know the Father. To walk in Him is to live in light. To be rooted in Him is to be complete.

Application

1. **Hope anchors the Christian life.** Faith and love grow from hope. If our hope shifts from heaven to earth, our faith will falter and our love will dry up. Keep your eyes on the inheritance laid up in heaven.

2. **The gospel bears fruit before full understanding.** God's Word begins working in the heart the moment it is heard. Don't lose heart if you see no immediate response—the seed of truth is alive, and God gives the increase in His time.

3. **Knowledge must lead to wisdom.** Biblical learning is not meant to fill notebooks but to transform lives. To know God's will is to live it.

4. **Power is given for perseverance.** God strengthens His people not to make life easy, but to make them steadfast. True strength is

measured in patience, faithfulness, and joy under pressure.

5. **Christ must remain central.** Every philosophy, ritual, or experience that tries to add to Christ ends up subtracting from Him. He is not part of our faith—He is our faith. The more we understand who He is, the less we will crave anything else.

Prayer

Father, we thank Thee for Thy Son, the image of the invisible God, the Creator and Redeemer of all things.

With the Spirit, we praise Thee for the power that holds the universe together and yet dwells in us.

Teach us to walk worthy of Thee—to be patient in trial, fruitful in service, and joyful in hope.

Root us deeply in the all-sufficient Christ, that our lives may bear fruit that endures.

We ask this in the name of Jesus, who is before all things and by whom all things consist.

Amen.

2

Christ in You: The Hope of Glory

Colossians 1:21–29

Paul began his letter by declaring the supremacy of Christ over all creation—the visible and the invisible, heaven and earth, the Church and the cosmos. Christ is not one among many divine figures; He is "the image of the invisible God, the firstborn of every creature." All things were created by Him, through Him, and for Him. Every atom in the universe holds together by His sustaining will.

But after lifting our eyes to behold His glory, Paul turns our gaze to the wonder of grace—that such a God should stoop to reconcile sinners to Himself. He now moves from cosmic theology to personal redemption, from the grandeur of the universe to the condition of the human heart. Verse 21 begins, "And you, that were sometime alienated and enemies in your mind by wicked works, yet now hath He reconciled."

Before we came to Christ, we were strangers—not that God was unaware of us, but that He had no relationship with us. His omniscience meant He knew every detail of our lives: our thoughts, our habits, our sins, our secret motives. Yet though He knew about us, we were not His. The difference between being known by God and being known to God is the difference between life and death.

Strangers and the False Security of Works

Jesus illustrated this in Matthew 7:21–23, where many stand before Him saying, "Lord, Lord, have we not prophesied in Thy name? and in Thy name have cast out devils? and in Thy name done many wonderful works?" They bring their works as evidence of acceptance, as though salvation could be proven by résumé. But the Lord's response is devastating: "I never knew you: depart from Me."

Notice His words—not *"I once knew you and forgot,"* but *"I never knew you."* There had never been a **relationship**, only **performance**. They had done things **for** God, but never **with** God. Their confidence rested on their activity, not intimacy. Their hope was in what they did in His name rather than who they were in His presence.

It is possible to live *near* the things of God, to speak His words, to serve His Church, and still remain a stranger to His heart. Religious motion is not the same as spiritual life. The Pharisees were masters of religious performance, but Jesus said they honored God with their lips while their hearts were far from Him. Fellowship with God cannot be earned by service—it can only be born of surrender.

Salvation, therefore, is not God discovering new information about us; it is God beginning a new relationship with us. It is the moment when the Judge becomes our Father and the Creator becomes our Redeemer. Before Christ, we were known as rebels under wrath; in Christ, we are known as children under grace. Knowledge about God may impress men, but only relationship with God transforms the soul.

Paul says we were not only strangers but enemies— "in your minds by wicked works." Sin is not first an action but a condition. We do not become sinners because we sin; we sin because we are sinners. Our rebellion begins in the mind and expresses itself in behavior. Sin is the outward evidence of inward alienation. The heart of man is not neutral toward God; it is naturally hostile. Every act of pride, every impulse of self-rule, is proof of that enmity.

Enemies in the Mind

Paul continues, "and enemies in your mind by wicked works." The barrier between man and God does not begin in the body—it begins in the mind. Our greatest problem is not ignorance but independence. We are not estranged from God because we know too little about Him, but because, knowing enough to honor Him, we choose instead to enthrone ourselves. The mind is the seat of our rebellion. Long before sin shows itself in the hands or the tongue, it takes root in the thoughts.

Romans 1 describes this inner rebellion with painful clarity: "Because that, when they knew God, they glorified Him not as God, neither were thankful; but became vain in their imaginations, and their foolish heart was darkened... Professing themselves to be wise, they became fools." (Romans 1:21–22) Humanity's fall was not the result of ignorance but arrogance. We knew God existed, yet we refused to acknowledge Him as Lord. We took what should have been worship and turned it into self-will. Our minds, created for truth, became factories of excuses; our reasoning, meant to mirror God's wisdom, became twisted to justify sin.

This is why Paul calls us enemies in our minds. Enmity is not merely a feeling of dislike toward God— it is an intellectual hostility, a willful decision to resist His rule. The sinner does not stumble accidentally into rebellion; he consciously chooses autonomy. He may cloak it in religion or philosophy, but beneath every form of godlessness lies the same declaration: "We will not have this Man to reign over us" (Luke 19:14).

This pride was the root of the Gnostic heresy infecting Colossae. The false teachers claimed enlightenment, insisting that through deeper understanding they could ascend to divine perfection. But in claiming to be wise, they repeated the error of Romans 1. They exalted intellect over obedience and turned knowledge into idolatry. They thought the mind could be a ladder to God, when in reality it had become the very wall that shut them out.

True wisdom begins not with discovery but with surrender. "The fear of the Lord is the beginning of wisdom." (Proverbs 9:10). Repentance, in the Greek *metanoia*, means literally "a change of mind." Salvation starts when the mind bows—when we stop explaining away sin and begin agreeing with God about it. Until that surrender happens, the war continues. The mind that refuses to yield to truth will always invent lies to protect its pride.

Our alienation, then, is not caused by lack of information but by lack of submission. The cure is not education but regeneration. The gospel does not simply inform the mind—it transforms it. The very mind that once plotted rebellion becomes the temple of the living Christ. Where once we devised excuses, now we discern truth. The battleground of thought becomes a sanctuary of peace. The enmity of the old mind gives way to "the mind of Christ," in which love, humility, and obedience flow freely from grace.

Reconciled Through His Body

Here Paul directly confronts the early Gnostic philosophy taking root in Colossae. The Gnostics taught that the physical body was evil and that the spiritual realm alone was pure. To them, salvation meant escaping the body through secret knowledge. Paul reverses the equation: the problem is not the body, but the mind; and salvation is not escape from flesh, but redemption through the incarnate body of Christ.

> *"Yet now hath He reconciled you in the body of His flesh through death." (v. 22)*

The Gnostics imagined a purely spiritual Christ, but Paul insists on the reality of His physical humanity. It was in a real body that He suffered, bled, and died. God used the very thing man despised—the material, mortal flesh—to bring salvation to the world. In doing so, Christ turned the enemy, death, into a servant. The last enemy became the instrument of our deliverance.

Through His death, Christ presents us "holy and unblameable and unreproveable in His sight." We who were once rebels are now consecrated as saints. We who were stained are declared spotless. We who were guilty stand blameless before the throne. This is our position in Christ—complete, secure, and judicially clean. We still sin, but we no longer stand condemned. Our failures may break fellowship, but never relationship.

When we sin as believers, we do not cease to be children of God; we simply lose the joy of His fellowship. As with an earthly parent and child, the bond remains, but the communion suffers until confession restores it. That is why 1 John 1:9 is so precious: "If we confess our sins, He is faithful and just to forgive us our sins, and to cleanse us from all unrighteousness." Restoration follows repentance, and fellowship follows forgiveness.

Grounded and Settled in Faith

Paul continues, "If ye continue in the faith grounded and settled, and be not moved away from the hope of the gospel." (Colossians 1:23)

At first glance, the conditional *if* can seem unsettling, as though the believer's standing depends on personal endurance. But Paul is not suggesting that salvation is fragile—he is describing its evidence. True faith is not a spark that flickers and dies; it is a flame kindled by the Spirit that endures every wind.

Perseverance is not the price of redemption—it is the proof of it.

When Paul says, "grounded and settled," he uses architectural imagery. The word grounded (Greek *themelioō*) refers to a foundation laid deep and firm, and settled (*hedraios*) describes something immovable, stable under pressure. Faith, then, is not a passing emotion or a momentary decision; it is a structure built on the solid bedrock of Christ Himself. Jesus used the same image in Matthew 7, contrasting the house built on sand with the one built on rock. The storms will come, but only one remains standing—the one founded on obedience to His word.

Paul's warning is timely because the Colossians were surrounded by philosophies that promised new enlightenment and higher experience. False teachers whispered that faith in Christ was only the beginning —that spiritual fullness required secret knowledge, mystical experiences, or adherence to ritual law. To these subtle temptations Paul responds: Be not moved away from the hope of the gospel. Do not trade gold for gravel. Everything you need for life and godliness is already found in Christ.

Faith, hope, and love—Paul's triad of Christian maturity—are all at work here. Faith roots us; hope anchors us; love steadies us. Faith reaches back to the finished work of Christ, hope looks forward to His promised glory, and love reaches outward to others in service. The believer who continues in these does not cling to salvation by willpower but stands firm by grace.

Paul's heart in this verse beats with pastoral concern. He had seen too many who professed faith only to fall away when trials arose. Like the shallow soil in Jesus' parable, their roots never reached the water. Their faith was a season, not a life. The apostle calls his readers to be **rooted**—to let their trust sink deep into the truth of who Christ is and what He has done. The deeper the root, the steadier the tree.

The phrase "moved away" carries the idea of being shifted from one place to another, like a boat unmoored and drifting from the harbor. A believer may face doubts, storms, and pressures, but the true anchor of the soul—Christ Himself—holds firm beneath the surface. We do not keep ourselves saved; we are kept by the power of God through faith. The call to remain is not a threat—it is an invitation to stability, to stay where grace has planted us.

The Christian who abides in the gospel finds that endurance is not a grim duty but a joyful confidence. The same power that reconciled us through the body of His flesh now sustains us in the life of His Spirit. We stand, not by striving, but by resting in the immovable hope of the gospel.

The Gospel Proclaimed and the Minister Transformed

Paul concludes this section with a sweeping statement:

"This gospel has been proclaimed in all creation under heaven, and of which I, Paul, am made a minister." (1:23b)

The gospel, by its very nature, refuses confinement. It began in a small upper room in Jerusalem, but within a single generation it had spread across the world—southward into Egypt and Africa, eastward through Syria and Persia, westward to Greece, Rome, and perhaps even as far as the British Isles. Wherever human language could be spoken, the name of Jesus was being carried. The same power that reconciles the soul also compels the witness. The gospel that takes root in a believer cannot remain silent—it bears fruit in testimony.

Paul himself was living evidence of that transforming power. Once, he had hunted believers with relentless zeal, breathing out threats and imprisonments against the Church of God. His was not a casual unbelief; it was militant hostility. Yet the light that blinded him on the Damascus Road also opened his eyes to grace. The persecutor became the preacher; the accuser became the ambassador. The man who once sought

36

to silence the name of Christ now spent his life making it known.

To say that Paul "became a minister" is not to say he chose a profession; it is to say he surrendered to a calling. The word minister (*diakonos*) means "servant," one who acts at the will of another. Paul was not a volunteer in God's service—he was a vessel claimed by divine appointment. The grace that saved him also assigned him. His ministry was not self-promotion but stewardship. He understood that to be reconciled to God is to be enlisted in His purpose.

There is profound irony in God's choice of this man. The gospel Paul once tried to destroy became the message he could not stop proclaiming. In God's redemptive economy, no zeal is wasted—only redirected. The same intensity that fueled his persecution now fueled his mission. Grace did not erase his passion; it sanctified it.

Through Paul, we see the great pattern of the redeemed: forgiven enemies become faithful witnesses. The one who was reconciled becomes a reconciler; the one who was pursued by mercy becomes the pursuer of souls. And so, when Paul says the gospel has gone out into all creation, he is not boasting of human effort but marveling at divine momentum. The message itself is alive. The Word that once spoke creation into being now speaks new creation into hearts.

Joy in the Midst of Suffering

Paul continues:

"Now I rejoice in my sufferings for you, and fill up in my flesh what is lacking in the afflictions of Christ, for the sake of His body, which is the church." (1:24)

It is one of the most astonishing statements in all his letters—*I rejoice in my sufferings*. These are not the words of a man who has lost touch with reality; they are the testimony of one who has found a deeper one. Paul wrote from a Roman prison, bruised, chained, and forgotten by many who once followed him. Yet joy, not despair, was his companion. For Paul, suffering was not an interruption of ministry—it was ministry.

The phrase "I fill up in my flesh what is lacking in the afflictions of Christ" has puzzled many readers. It does not mean that Christ's atonement was incomplete. His suffering on the cross was entirely sufficient for salvation. Nothing can be added to the finished work of Calvary. What Paul means is that he is sharing in the continuing cost of carrying Christ's message to a hostile world. The Head suffered once for sin; the body continues to suffer for the sake of His name.

Paul's wounds were not redemptive—they were representative. The servant bears in his body the marks of his Master. Every missionary, every faithful witness who endures rejection, persecution, or hardship for the gospel participates in this same pattern: Christ's suffering continues in His people until the work of redemption reaches every corner of creation.

When Paul says he rejoices, he is not rejoicing *because* of pain, but *within* it. His joy is not born from comfort but from calling. Suffering for the sake of Christ confirmed to Paul that he belonged to Christ. The chains that bound him to a Roman guard were, in his eyes, golden links binding him to the Lord's own heart. Each hardship became a reminder that he was sharing in the fellowship of His sufferings (Philippians 3:10).

Suffering, for the believer, is never wasted. When it is endured for Christ's sake, it becomes seed that bears eternal fruit. Paul saw his imprisonment as an investment: through his suffering, the gospel was being strengthened, believers were being encouraged, and Christ was being magnified. As he wrote elsewhere, "The things which happened unto me have fallen out rather unto the furtherance of the gospel" (Philippians 1:12).

The modern church often seeks to avoid discomfort, but Paul teaches that true ministry always carries a cross. The measure of Christ's power in a life is not seen in how much we escape suffering, but in how we endure it. Joy in affliction is not denial—it is devotion. It is the proof that something greater than pain has taken root within us.

Paul's example reminds us that every hardship endured for the gospel becomes a continuation of Christ's presence in the world. When the church suffers with grace, the world sees Jesus again. The believer's wounds become witnesses of the Savior's work.

As a servant of the Church, Paul sees himself as a steward of divine revelation—entrusted to "complete the word of God." Through Paul's pen, the mystery hidden for ages was made known. He writes, "The mystery which hath been hid from ages and generations, but now is made manifest to His saints." (v. 26)

What is this mystery? "**Christ in you, the hope of glory.**" (v. 27)

The Old Testament saints looked for the coming of Messiah, but they could not fathom that the very life of God would one day dwell within believers. The prophets anticipated the reign of the King; the apostles experienced the indwelling of the King Himself. The divine glory that once filled the tabernacle now resides in the hearts of His people. The word "glory" (*doxa*) carries the idea of radiance— of shining forth. Christ in us is the light within the lamp, the glow of grace transforming clay vessels into vessels of honor.

"We proclaim Him," Paul writes, "warning every man, and teaching every man in all wisdom, that we may present every man perfect in Christ Jesus." (v. 28)

The goal of ministry is maturity—believers fully grown, bearing fruit that unmistakably reveals their identity. A tree is known by its fruit; a Christian is known by the likeness of Christ. Maturity is not measured by knowledge or position but by resemblance to the Savior. The more Christ dwells richly within us, the more our lives reflect His character—love, joy, peace, longsuffering, gentleness, and faith.

> *"Whereunto I also labour, striving according to His working, which worketh in me mightily." (v. 29)*

Paul's labor is real, but the power behind it is divine. He is not a spiritual spectator but an active participant in God's redemptive mission. His ministry demands every ounce of effort—study, prayer, travel, preaching, writing, and suffering—but even this exertion is fueled by something beyond himself. He works, yet it is God who works in him.

This is the mystery of Christian service: human weakness harnessed by divine strength. The same power that raised Jesus from the dead courses through His people, making ordinary men and women instruments of eternal purpose. Paul does not boast of endurance; he boasts of enablement. The ministry is not sustained by human energy but by Christ's indwelling strength—the inexhaustible might of the risen Lord operating through frail vessels.

To labor "according to His working" means to move in step with God's activity, not to run ahead of it or lag behind it. The servant's striving becomes sacred when it harmonizes with the Master's will. Every sermon prepared, every visit made, every prayer offered in the Spirit becomes part of Christ's continuing work on earth. The believer's effort, rightly aligned, is not wasted toil—it is resurrection power in motion.

This same power is at work in us. The Christian life is not a call to exhaustion but to cooperation—to yield our weakness to His strength and our effort to His energy. Every believer, no matter how ordinary their sphere, becomes a vessel of divine activity. When we serve, teach, comfort, forgive, or endure, it is not merely we who labor—it is Christ working mightily within us. Our responsibility is faithfulness; the results belong to Him. The labor that begins in surrender ends in strength.

Summary

This passage moves us from the majesty of Christ to the mystery of Christ—from who He is in heaven to who He is within us.

- Once we were strangers and enemies; now we are sons and saints.

- Once we were alienated in our minds; now we are reconciled through His body.

- Once we were condemned by sin; now we are clothed in holiness.

The central truth is this: Christ in you is the hope of glory. The same Lord who reigns above the heavens now lives within the believer. His presence is not symbolic but real, not distant but personal. The life of Christ is the power that sustains our obedience, transforms our character, and assures our future. Salvation is not merely rescue from sin—it is union with the Savior.

Application

Reconciliation begins with relationship. God does not merely forgive; He restores. Salvation is not a transaction but a transformation—moving us from strangers to sons.

1. **Sin is a symptom, not the disease.** Our problem is not behavior but nature. We sin because we are sinners. Only Christ can change what we are at the core.

2. **True faith perseveres.** Shallow belief withers under pressure. Rooted faith endures because its hope is anchored in Christ, not circumstances.

3. **The gospel demands change.** You cannot add Christ to your old life and remain the same. When Christ moves in, everything else must move out.

4. **Christ in you is sufficient.** The indwelling Christ is not a portion of God's presence but the fullness of it. Whatever you face, the One who holds all things together holds you.

5. **Maturity is the goal of ministry.** Growth is not optional—it is the natural result of life. A faith that never grows may not be alive.

Prayer

Father,

*we thank Thee for the mystery revealed—
Christ in us, the hope of glory.*

*With the Spirit, we rejoice that Thou hast
reconciled us through the body of Thy Son,
turning enemies into heirs and sinners into
saints.*

*Teach us to walk in the light of this truth, to
live as those indwelt by Christ Himself.*

*Strengthen us to persevere in faith, to bear
fruit worthy of Thee, and to shine with the
glory that dwells within.*

*We ask this in the name of Jesus, who lives in
us and through us forever.*

Amen.

Rooted

3

Rooted in Christ

Paul's Pastoral Conflict and the Guardrails of Grace

"As ye have therefore received Christ Jesus the Lord, so walk ye in him: Rooted and built up in him, and stablished in the faith, as ye have been taught, abounding therein with thanksgiving." (Colossians 2:6–7)

The second chapter of Colossians moves from Paul's soaring vision of Christ's supremacy into the believer's daily experience of walking in that truth. Having exalted Christ as "the image of the invisible God" (1:15) and the Head of the body, Paul now calls the church to live in a way that corresponds to that confession—to walk as those truly rooted in Him.

Paul's heart for this church was intense. Though he had never visited Colossae, he wrote with the affection of a shepherd who labors for the health of his flock. Epaphras, who likely founded the church after hearing Paul's preaching in Ephesus, had reported to him from Rome about the believers in the Lycus Valley. Some were growing strong, but others were being lured by false teachers—men who combined Jewish ritualism, Greek philosophy, and mystical visions into a dangerous counterfeit gospel.

Paul's concern was not merely intellectual; he says, "I would that ye knew what great conflict I have for you" (v. 1). His struggle was prayerful and pastoral. He wrestled for them in spirit—interceding as Epaphras did "always labouring fervently… that ye may stand perfect and complete in all the will of God" (4:12)—and he contended through the written Word that God was using him to produce for their defense (cf. 4:16). Paul's labor was to give the church Scriptural guardrails: not bars for a cage, but rails along a mountain road—grace-built boundaries that keep travelers from the precipice while they move forward in freedom. He knew that "all scripture is given by inspiration of God… that the man of God may be perfect, throughly furnished unto all good works" (2 Tim. 3:16–17). Thus he wrote, preached, prayed, and suffered, not to burden tender consciences with traditions of men, but to anchor them to Christ, "whom we preach... that we may present every man perfect in Christ Jesus" (1:28).

These guardrails protect liberty, not legalism. They do not hem the church into human customs; they hem the church out of deception. False teaching sounds reasonable (2:4), but Scripture exposes its hollowness and redirects the heart to the fullness that is in Christ (2:8–10). Paul's aim, then, was a congregation both knit together in love and kept together by truth — hearts encouraged, minds established, and lives guided by the Word, so that the saints might walk safely and steadily until they reach the summit: the glory of Christ.

Full Assurance in the Knowledge of Christ

He longed that their hearts would be "comforted, being knit together in love," and that they might come to "all riches of the full assurance of understanding" (v. 2). The word assurance translates the Greek term πληροφορία (plērophoria), which literally means full carrying or complete confidence. It conveys the image of a vessel so filled that it is ready for its voyage — nothing lacking, nothing uncertain. Spiritually, it describes a heart fully persuaded, carried forward by conviction rather than tossed by doubt.

This is not a shallow optimism or emotional certainty; it is the deep, Spirit-born persuasion that arises from knowing Christ rightly. The believer's assurance grows in proportion to his grasp of Christ's sufficiency. When Paul speaks of "the full assurance of understanding," he links *plērophoria* to *epignōsis*—a precise and relational knowledge of Christ. The two are inseparable: knowledge fuels confidence, and confidence steadies obedience.

Paul's prayer, then, is that their hearts would be strengthened—not by mere comfort, but by conviction —and "knit together in love." Unity in the body of Christ flows from shared understanding of the Son of God. As the truth of Christ fills the mind, love binds the hearts. Doctrine and devotion meet here: sound theology producing sound fellowship.

And from that unity springs assurance. The more the believer beholds Christ—the incarnate fullness of deity—the more certain his footing becomes. The storms of life may shake the branches, but they cannot move the roots. Assurance is not self-confidence but Christ-confidence—a steady trust anchored in the One who holds all things together. To know Him is to rest; to rest in Him is to stand firm.

Christ, the Treasure House of All Wisdom

When Paul declares that "in Him are hid all the treasures of wisdom and knowledge," he is not describing abstract ideas but the very nature of reality itself. Christ is not merely the Revealer of truth—He is Truth personified. He said, "I am the way, the truth, and the life" (John 14:6). Truth is not a concept to be mastered but a Person to be known. Every fact, every principle, every law that rightly describes the world finds its coherence in Him.

From the opening words of Genesis, Christ—the eternal Word—established reality by His proclamation: "And God said..." (Gen. 1). The universe exists because He spoke; order, beauty, and meaning flow from His voice. What we call "natural law" is simply the echo of His decrees still resonating through creation. "By Him were all things created... and by Him all things consist" (Col. 1:16–17). The galaxies hold their courses because the Word still holds His breath.

Every field of study, rightly pursued, leads back to its Source. The mathematician traces His precision, the artist mirrors His beauty, the scientist observes His handiwork. As Isaac Newton once wrote, "In the absence of any other proof, the thumb alone would convince me of God's existence." Genuine science does not erase the need for faith; it magnifies it. The more deeply we explore the created order, the more clearly we perceive the wisdom of the Creator.

Wisdom, then, is truth in motion—truth applied toward the right end. Knowledge fills the mind; understanding shapes perception; but wisdom directs both toward the glory of God. That is why Scripture says, "The fear of the LORD is the beginning of wisdom" (Prov. 9:10). Reverence, not intellect, is the foundation of true insight. To fear God is to recognize reality as it truly is: created, sustained, and defined by Him. All truth, from the structure of atoms to the order of angels, calls out His glory.

When we bring our learning under His lordship, wisdom ceases to be an achievement and becomes an act of worship. Every discovery, every application of knowledge, becomes a way of saying, "Thine is the kingdom, and the power, and the glory." To know Christ is to see the world as it truly is—to see light in His light, and to live so that truth itself brings praise to its Source.

Paul says that these treasures are "hid in Christ"—the word translated hid is ἀπόκρυφος (apokruphos), meaning kept safe, laid up, or stored away for preservation. It does not mean hidden in the sense of concealed from sight, but hidden as something precious is guarded until the appointed time. The treasures of divine wisdom are not locked away to frustrate seekers; they are preserved in Christ to be revealed to those who are His. What was once veiled in shadow through types and prophecies now stands unveiled in the face of Jesus Christ. The "mystery" Paul so often mentions is not a puzzle to be solved but a Person to be known. In Him, the concealed becomes clear.

This sense of *apokruphos* also underscores the exclusivity of Christ as the repository of all truth. The world's systems may offer fragments of knowledge, but the fullness is kept in Him. Outside of Christ, men search endlessly through speculation; in Christ, revelation is made plain. As Paul wrote earlier, "Even the mystery which hath been hid from ages and from generations, but now is made manifest to his saints" (1:26). The treasures are hidden not to exclude the humble but to expose the proud—hidden from the wise in their own eyes and revealed to those who approach in faith.

Beware of Captivity Through Human Philosophy

Thus Paul warns, "Beware lest any man spoil you through philosophy and vain deceit, after the tradition of men, after the rudiments of the world, and not after Christ" (v. 8). The word spoil (Greek *sulagōgeō*) literally means to carry off as plunder. It paints the picture of a victorious army parading its captives through the streets—bound, humiliated, and stripped of freedom. False doctrine does exactly that. It kidnaps the mind and drags the heart from its anchor in Christ, turning liberated believers into prisoners of human thought.

The danger is rarely obvious. Paul says deception comes through "philosophy and vain deceit"—ideas that sound refined, even reasonable. Philosophy, from *phileo* (to love) and *sophia* (wisdom), simply means "the love of wisdom." There is nothing inherently wrong in that; indeed, all true wisdom belongs to God. But when human speculation becomes detached from divine revelation, the love of wisdom becomes the worship of the mind. The pursuit of truth without the fear of God becomes vanity dressed as virtue.

He further warns that these systems are "after the tradition of men" and "after the rudiments of the world." The word rudiments (Greek *stoicheia*) refers to the "basic elements" or "elemental principles" of the world—the alphabet of fallen reasoning. It describes the framework of thought that governs human culture apart from God: self-sufficiency, pride, achievement, and merit. These are the gravitational pulls of the old nature, always drawing the soul away from grace. Every false system of thought—whether religious legalism or secular humanism—shares this same root: it exalts man and marginalizes Christ.

By Paul's day, the glory of Greek philosophy had already faded into decadence. The age of Plato and

Rooted

Aristotle had given way to idle disputants who multiplied words but produced nothing of substance. Athens, once the fountainhead of learning, had become a theater for spectacle. Philosophers gathered not to pursue truth but to perform it. They sat in colonnades and courtyards spinning theories that neither fed the hungry nor changed a single heart. Their endless disputations—Stoic, Epicurean, Cynic, and Skeptic—had devolved into little more than intellectual entertainment. The marketplace buzzed with opinion, but the world remained empty of wisdom.

Luke's account in Acts 17 captures the spirit of the time: "For all the Athenians and strangers which were there spent their time in nothing else, but either to tell, or to hear some new thing." They loved novelty more than truth. The search for wisdom had become entertainment. Philosophy had grown comfortable in its confusion—brilliant minds walking in circles, endlessly debating reality while standing blind before the God who made it.

It is not hard to see the parallel in our own age. The world is once again crowded with "talking heads"—men and women who fill airwaves and feeds with opinion, outrage, and speculation. Our culture prizes argument over understanding, style over substance, noise over knowledge. The modern philosopher has traded the agora for the screen, yet the spirit is the same: endless discussion without direction, analysis without awe, ideas without incarnation. We have become a society that entertains itself with truth but never bows before it.

Paul's warning is timeless: beware of being "spoiled" by such noise. Empty reasoning still plunders the soul. When thought is severed from worship, wisdom dies and only chatter remains. But when Christ is the center of our thinking, knowledge regains its dignity and words recover their weight. The Christian's task is not to abandon thought but to redeem it—to bring every argument captive to Christ, the Truth who cannot be out-reasoned and will not be dethroned.

The Fullness of Christ

Paul now sets the emptiness of worldly speculation against the overwhelming fullness of divine reality: "For in Him dwelleth all the fulness of the Godhead bodily. And ye are complete in Him, which is the head of all principality and power." (vv. 9–10)

Here is the heart of the Colossian letter. Against every counterfeit philosophy, Paul lifts Christ—not merely as a wise man or moral teacher, but as the incarnate dwelling place of all that God is. The word fulness (Greek plērōma) was a favorite term among the false teachers of Paul's day, especially the early Gnostics, who taught that divine fullness was scattered among many spiritual beings. Paul reclaims their language and corrects their theology in one breath: the *plērōma* is not divided—it is concentrated in Christ alone. Every attribute of Deity, every power, every perfection, every purpose of God is embodied in Him.

> **Plērōma**
>
> *fullness or completeness, especially that which fills something to its intended capacity. In Colossians, Paul uses the term to insist that all the fullness of God dwells in Christ, leaving nothing lacking and nothing to be supplemented.*

And this fullness "dwelleth" in Him bodily. The word means "to make its permanent home." It was not a temporary visitation of divinity, nor a symbolic expression of it. In Christ, the eternal Word took up full residence in human flesh. The invisible became visible; the transcendent took form. The God who cannot be contained by heaven chose to be contained in a man. This is the mystery of the Incarnation—the fullness of God inhabiting a body so that the fullness of grace might inhabit ours.

But Paul does not stop with Christ's sufficiency; he extends it to ours. "Ye are complete in Him." The verb (*plēroō*) carries the same root as *plērōma*—the idea of being filled to the brim. What the false teachers sought through secret knowledge or ritual performance, the believer already possesses in union with Christ. The Christian does not live from emptiness seeking to be filled, but from fullness overflowing into obedience. We are not climbing toward completion; we are living out of it.

That completeness also defines our standing in the spiritual realm: "which is the head of all principality and power." Every created authority—angelic or earthly, visible or invisible—stands beneath His command. The same powers that once held the Gentile world in bondage are now subject to the risen Christ. He is not merely first among equals; He is Lord over all. Therefore, no philosophy, no system, no spiritual hierarchy can add to what believers already have in Him. To look elsewhere for spiritual strength is to step away from the throne itself.

In a world obsessed with achieving, Paul reminds us that grace begins with being filled. The believer's task is not to strive for what he lacks, but to live out what he has been given. Christ is not an accessory to our spirituality; He is its source, its substance, and its satisfaction. The answer to every deficiency is not more effort, more knowledge, or more experience—it is more of Christ.

And this spiritual reality is pictured in baptism: "Buried with him in baptism, wherein also ye are risen with him through the faith of the operation of God, who hath raised him from the dead" (v. 12). Baptism is not a work that saves, but a witness that proclaims—we have died with Christ and have been raised to new life in Him. It is the believer's visible testimony that the past is buried and a new creation has begun.

Buried and Raised with Christ

"And you, being dead in your sins and the uncircumcision of your flesh, hath he quickened together with him, having forgiven you all trespasses." (v. 13)

The outward act of baptism portrays the inward miracle of regeneration. What the water signifies, grace performs. Paul now turns from symbol to substance—from the believer's public witness to the divine operation that makes it true. Before faith laid hold of Christ, we were dead in our sins—spiritually lifeless, unable to respond, untouched by the impulses of divine life. Death in Scripture never means extinction, but separation: the soul existing apart from the life of God, alienated from His fellowship and indifferent to His call.

Yet into that spiritual death the voice of Christ sounded, as once He called to Lazarus from the tomb. The same power that raised Jesus from the grave raised us from guilt to grace. We were not improved, but made alive. We did not climb toward God; God stooped to us. Salvation is not moral renovation but resurrection—He hath quickened us together with Him. The believer's life is the shared life of the risen Lord. His pulse beats in our spirit; His righteousness covers our guilt; His victory becomes our standing.

And this new life rests upon a single, magnificent fact: having forgiven you all trespasses. The tense is decisive and complete. Forgiveness is not progressive but finished. Every sin, every failure, every debt of the past has been canceled by the cross. The believer does not live on probation but in pardon.

Paul then describes how that pardon was secured:

The Cross: Our Debt Erased, Our Enemies Defeated

"Blotting out the handwriting of ordinances that was against us, which was contrary to us, and took it out of the way, nailing it to his cross." (v. 14)

The "handwriting of ordinances" was a legal term for a signed record of debt—a document in which the debtor confessed his obligation in his own hand. Under the Law, that record stood as an unanswerable witness against the sinner. Each commandment we broke added another line to the indictment; the whole Law was "contrary to us," for it demanded righteousness and could not supply it.

But at Calvary, that entire record was erased. The phrase *blotting out* means to wipe the writing from a tablet until no trace remains. Ancient ink did not cut into parchment but lay upon it, easily washed away with water. So Christ, by His blood, wiped away the testimony that condemned us. The debt has not merely been stamped "paid"; it has been taken out of the way—removed from the courtroom entirely.

And then Paul adds the crowning image: "nailing it to his cross." The Roman execution board often displayed the crime for which a man was condemned. Over Jesus hung the inscription, "This is the King of the Jews." Yet unseen by human eyes, another document was nailed there—the ledger of our guilt. Every charge, every transgression, every violation of divine law was fastened to the wood and paid in full. The hammer that struck His hands drove our debt into oblivion.

Thus, what was once a symbol of shame became the monument of mercy. The cross is both altar and archive—the place where sin was judged and the record destroyed.

The Cross: Our Debt Erased, Our Enemies Defeated

"And having spoiled principalities and powers, he made a shew of them openly, triumphing over them in it." (v. 15)

Here Paul moves from the courtroom to the battlefield. The word spoiled means "to strip off" or "to disarm." Through His death and resurrection, Christ stripped the spiritual rulers of darkness of their claim against the redeemed. The weapons of accusation were torn from their grasp; the handwriting of ordinances that armed them has been removed. What looked like defeat was divine conquest.

In the ancient world, a victorious general returned home in a public procession, his captives marching behind him—stripped, subdued, and displayed as trophies of triumph. Paul uses that image deliberately. Christ, having triumphed over the powers of evil, paraded them in open disgrace. The very cross on which He was condemned became His chariot of victory.

This is the great paradox of redemption: the moment of Christ's deepest humiliation was the hour of His greatest glory. The rulers of darkness thought they had overthrown the Son of God; instead, He overthrew their dominion. They nailed Him to a tree, but He nailed their accusations there with Him. They raised Him up to mock Him, but in being lifted up He drew all men unto Himself.

At the cross, sin was canceled, the Law was satisfied, and Satan was disarmed. The believer stands not beneath condemnation but within conquest. The war has been won, the debt erased, the captives freed.

Shadows and Substance: Liberty from Legalism

"Let no man therefore judge you in meat, or in drink, or in respect of an holyday, or of the new moon, or of the sabbath days: which are a shadow of things to come; but the body is of Christ." (vv. 16–17)

Because the cross has canceled our debt and conquered our enemies, Paul now draws the practical conclusion: "Let no man therefore judge you." The *therefore* rests on Calvary. Since Christ has fulfilled the Law, no human tribunal may bind the believer with ordinances that grace has rendered obsolete.

The Colossian heresy combined Jewish ritualism with pagan mysticism, teaching that spiritual maturity came through dietary restrictions, holy days, and ceremonial observances. These things had a venerable history—given originally by God through Moses—but their purpose was preparatory, not perpetual. They pointed forward to Christ. Once the substance arrived, the shadow lost its authority.

The word *judge* carries the sense of condemning or disqualifying. False teachers were sitting in self-appointed courts, pronouncing verdicts on those who did not conform to their system of scruples. Paul says in effect, "Do not submit to their jurisdiction; your standing is in Christ, not in ceremony." The Christian's diet, calendar, and ritual practice are not the measure of holiness; the measure is Christ Himself.

Paul lists the familiar categories of Jewish observance: meat or drink—the dietary laws of Leviticus; holyday—the annual feasts; new moon—the monthly offerings; and sabbath days—the weekly rest. These were divinely ordained shadows, cast backward from the substance that was to come. Each feast, each ordinance, each sabbath pointed to Him. The Passover anticipated His sacrifice; the Feast of Firstfruits foreshadowed His resurrection; the Day of Atonement prefigured His intercession; the Sabbath itself whispered of the rest found in His finished work.

But when the light of Christ dawned, the shadows fled. To cling to the ceremonial after Calvary is to turn one's back to the sunrise. The Law served as a tutor leading us to Christ (Gal. 3:24); now that the lesson has been fulfilled, the tutor steps aside.

When Paul says, "but the body is of Christ," he contrasts shadow with substance. The word body here means reality or fulfillment—the solid form that casts the shadow. Christ is that reality. The festivals, foods, and sabbaths were outlines on the page of prophecy; He is the living Person who fills them in. To measure spirituality by such externals is to trade substance for silhouette.

The danger Paul confronts is subtle. Legalism seldom presents itself as rebellion; it masquerades as reverence. It begins with a desire to honor God and ends by replacing grace with rules. It promises depth and produces division. By making conformity the test of holiness, it shifts the focus from Christ's sufficiency to human performance. The result is bondage disguised as devotion.

But the gospel calls believers to rest in a finished redemption. Our acceptance before God is not maintained by dietary caution or liturgical precision but by the righteousness of Christ. To let others judge us in these things is to forget that the Judge Himself has already pronounced us righteous in His Son.

The believer, then, walks in liberty—not the liberty of license, but the liberty of love. Freed from condemnation, he is free to serve. The Law's shadows have found their light; the ceremonies have found their Christ. All that remains is gratitude, not guilt.

The Mirage of False Humility and Angel Worship

"Let no man beguile you of your reward in a voluntary humility and worshipping of angels, intruding into those things which he hath not seen, vainly puffed up by his fleshly mind, and not holding the Head, from which all the body by joints and bands having nourishment ministered, and knit together, increaseth with the increase of God." (vv. 18–19)

Having exposed the emptiness of legalism, Paul now warns against its twin deception—false mysticism. If the first exalts rules above Christ, the second exalts experience above Christ. Both have the same root: pride disguised as piety.

The apostle's phrase, "Let no man beguile you of your reward," literally means to act as an umpire against you—to declare you disqualified from the prize. The false teachers were doing just that, claiming that ordinary believers could never reach spiritual fullness without adopting their regimen of visions, mediators, and ascetic practices. Paul insists that such men have already stepped outside the boundary lines of truth.

He describes them as practicing "a voluntary humility." The word seems noble—who would oppose humility? —yet Paul uses it ironically. This was humility performed, not possessed. It paraded self-abasement to earn admiration. The false teachers spoke softly, dressed plainly, and fasted often, but their modesty was theater. It was pride masquerading as meekness. Theirs was not submission to Christ, but a subtle competition with Him.

From that counterfeit humility flowed "the worshipping of angels." The Gnostic systems of Paul's day taught that God was too transcendent to be approached directly. Between God and man stood ranks of angelic intermediaries, and to reach the divine, one must venerate these lesser beings. Such devotion sounded reverent but in truth insulted the sufficiency of Christ. The One Mediator had been replaced by a hierarchy of substitutes.

The same danger lingers in every age. Whenever devotion is directed anywhere but to Christ—whether to saints, spirits, systems, or sensations—the heart drifts from its true center. The believer does not need a chain of intermediaries, for the chain has been broken. Through the blood of Christ, the veil is torn; the holiest place is open.

Paul further unmasks the psychology of this deception: such a man "intrudes into those things which he hath not seen, vainly puffed up by his fleshly mind." He pretends insight into hidden mysteries, claiming visions and revelations beyond the reach of common faith. His pride is cloaked in spiritual vocabulary, yet it is merely the flesh reaching for divine status. In the name of depth, he drowns in self delusion.

This self-made mysticism is the opposite of revelation. Instead of bowing before what God has spoken, it speculates about what God has not. The truly spiritual man does not climb ladders of imagination; he abides in the Word. The more a believer is filled with Christ, the less he feels the need to look beyond Him.

Paul concludes with the real issue: "and not holding the Head." The error is not primarily intellectual but relational. In seeking higher experiences, the false teachers had let go of Christ Himself. The Head is the source of all life and growth for the body. To lose connection with Him is to sever the nerve of vitality. Every system that detracts from His centrality—no matter how ornate or ancient—inevitably withers.

By contrast, those who hold fast to the Head are nourished and knit together. Life flows from Christ to every member of His body, just as blood circulates through veins and arteries. The Church grows, not by mystical speculation or external ceremony, but by the inward operation of divine life—"the increase of God." Real spirituality is not self-manufactured; it is God's own life expanding within His people.

Thus Paul's argument unfolds with perfect balance:

• Legalism dethrones Christ by replacing grace with rules.

- Mysticism dethrones Christ by replacing revelation with visions.

- Both end the same way—not holding the Head.

But the believer who abides in Christ needs neither. His humility is genuine because it grows from worship, not performance. His devotion is pure because it looks to the risen Lord, not to angels or apparitions. His growth is steady because it draws from the life of the Head.

Dead with Christ, Free from the World's Rudiments

"Wherefore if ye be dead with Christ from the rudiments of the world, why, as though living in the world, are ye subject to ordinances, (Touch not; taste not; handle not; which all are to perish with the using;) after the commandments and doctrines of men? Which things have indeed a shew of wisdom in will worship, and humility, and neglecting of the body; not in any honour to the satisfying of the flesh." (vv. 20–23)

Paul now draws the argument of this chapter to its solemn conclusion. Having shown that believers have been made alive with Christ, he reminds them that they have also died with Him—died to the world's elementary principles and to every system that once claimed to make them righteous. The Christian is not bound to climb a ladder to heaven; he has already been raised there in Christ. Therefore, to return to the world's religious machinery is to crawl back into the grave from which grace has freed him.

> ### Stoicheia
>
> *the basic principles or elemental systems that order life apart from Christ, whether religious, moral, or cosmic. In Colossians, Paul uses the term to describe structures that appear powerful or wise but ultimately enslave because they are not rooted in Christ.*

The rudiments of the world—the *stoicheia* Paul mentioned earlier—are the basic, earthly patterns of religion: doing to deserve, performing to please, restraining to redeem. These are the ABCs of human righteousness, the moral alphabet of every fallen creed. But in Christ, those rudiments have been rendered obsolete. The believer no longer lives under the tyranny of "do this and live," but under the liberty of "it is finished."

Paul's question pierces with holy logic: "Why, as though living in the world, are ye subject to ordinances?" If you have died with Christ, why act as though the old regime still holds authority over you? It is as though a freed prisoner keeps reporting to the warden each morning, begging permission to go about his day. The believer's chains have been broken; to live as though still bound is to deny the power of the cross.

The slogans of these false teachers—"Touch not; taste not; handle not"—sound devout, but they are the language of bondage. They define holiness by avoidance, not affection. They promise purity through deprivation, not transformation. The irony, Paul says, is that these very things "perish with the using." Their holiness expires on contact. They cannot touch the conscience; they only regulate the senses.

Such commandments are "after the doctrines of men." They may quote Scripture, but they twist it into law without grace. They carry the tone of heaven but the origin of earth. Every generation invents its own list of taboos—certain foods, dress codes, observances— meant to measure spirituality by conformity. Yet all these outward fences cannot keep sin from the heart. Religion can starve the body and still feed pride.

Paul grants that these practices "have indeed a shew of wisdom." They look impressive. They produce discipline, self-denial, and visible devotion. The apostle even names their threefold appeal:

• Will worship—the veneration of one's own resolve.

- Humility—a counterfeit modesty that draws attention to itself.

- Neglecting of the body—ascetic rigor mistaken for holiness.

But beneath that polished exterior lies futility. Such exercises are "not in any honour to the satisfying of the flesh." The phrase is difficult in English, but Paul's meaning is clear: these outward austerities do not conquer the flesh—they feed it. Pride thrives on self-imposed religion. The ascetic who glories in his deprivation is still self-centered; he has merely traded indulgence for vanity.

Here lies the tragedy of all man-made piety: it looks heavenward but grows from the soil of self. The cross alone crucifies the flesh. Only when a man dies with Christ does he find rest from striving and joy in obedience. The world says, "Deny yourself to become worthy." The gospel says, "You are accepted—now walk worthy." One begins with effort; the other begins with grace.

Thus, the chapter closes where it began: with Christ as the believer's completeness. The Colossians are called to turn from shadows to substance, from law to life, from effort to abiding. The One who nailed the handwriting of ordinances to His cross has no interest in watching His people nail new ones beside it. True holiness is not achieved by what we forbid ourselves, but by Who fills us.

Summary

Colossians 2 reveals the heart of the gospel's transforming power. Paul contends for the believers' stability against false philosophies and legalistic systems that promise spirituality apart from Christ. His message is simple and sweeping: Christ is sufficient.

In Him dwells all the fullness of God. In Him we are made complete. In Him the old life is cut away, the record of sin is destroyed, and the believer is raised to walk in newness of life.

No tradition, vision, or religious performance can improve upon that finished work. The shadow has served its purpose; the substance has come. Christ alone is the believer's righteousness, wisdom, and strength.

To be rooted in Christ is to draw life from His indwelling presence and to grow upward in the soil of His grace. Every rival claim to wisdom, every demand for works, every attempt to earn God's favor must wither in the light of His cross.

Application

Paul's warning to the Colossians remains vital in our day. The world still entices believers with philosophies that sound reasonable, spiritual systems that promise power, and religious habits that substitute for relationship.

We must remember: the Christian life begins and continues by faith. The same grace that saved us sustains us. We walk as we began—trusting, resting, abiding.

To be rooted in Christ means that our beliefs, decisions, and identity all draw nourishment from Him. The world's wisdom may seem clever, but its foundations are sand. Christ alone offers stability that endures the storm.

When you face spiritual confusion, return to the simplicity of verse six: "As ye have therefore received Christ Jesus the Lord, so walk ye in him." Live every day the same way you came to Him—by grace, through faith, out of love.

Guard your heart against anything that promises "something more" than Christ. You cannot improve upon the fullness you already possess. Let gratitude overflow. Let your roots sink deep.

You are circumcised with His cutting, buried in His death, raised in His resurrection, filled with His Spirit, and freed by His victory. You lack nothing in Him.

Prayer

Father,

We thank Thee for the completeness we have in Thy Son. We confess that too often we chase wisdom apart from Him, strength apart from grace, and peace apart from faith. Forgive our wandering hearts.

Teach us to walk as we were saved—trusting, thankful, and dependent upon Christ alone. Let our roots go deep into His Word, our minds be guarded from deception, and our lives be living testimonies of resurrection power.

With the Spirit, we pray in the name of Jesus Christ our Lord.

Amen.

Rooted

4

Clothed to Live

Colossians 3:1-11

Paul's letter to the Colossians now reaches a great turning point. Having lifted our eyes to see the supremacy of Christ in all things, he calls us to live as those who are united with Him. The truths of the first two chapters are not meant to remain in the clouds of theology; they descend now into the daily walk of the believer.

Paul writes:

> "If ye then be risen with Christ, seek those things which are above, where Christ sitteth on the right hand of God. Set your affection on things above, not on things on the earth. For ye

are dead, and your life is hid with Christ in God. When Christ, who is our life, shall appear, then shall ye also appear with him in glory." (Col. 3:1-4)

Paul opens chapter 3 with a conditional clause: "If ye then be risen with Christ..." (Col. 3:1). In English, if can sound tentative—as though our resurrection with Christ were uncertain. But Paul is using what grammarians call a first-class conditional: if (Greek ei) with an indicative verb, a construction that assumes the condition to be true for the sake of argument— indeed, in Paul's theology, true in fact.

A quick overview of the New Testament's common conditionals helps:

1. First-class (*ei* + indicative): assumes truth—"since this is so..." (e.g., Col. 3:1).

2. Second-class (*ei* + indicative in both protasis and apodosis, often with *an*): contrary to fact—"if this were so (but it isn't)..." (e.g., 1 Cor. 2:8).

3. Third-class (*ean* + subjunctive): probable/ contingent—"if this should happen..." (frequent in John's Gospel and 1 John).

4. Fourth-class (*ei* + optative, often with *an*): potential/less probable (rare in the NT; largely a classical form).

In Colossians 3:1 Paul uses first-class: *ei oun synēgerthēte*—"if (as in, since) you were raised with Christ." The verb is aorist passive indicative ("were raised"), pointing to a completed act God has already performed in the believer's union with Christ (cf. Col. 2:12; Rom. 6:4–5). Paul is not dangling a possibility but declaring a reality: you have been raised. Read idiomatically, the force is "Since you have been raised with Christ..."

This matters devotionally. The Christian life does not begin with a question mark but with an exclamation point. The imperatives that follow ("seek," "set your affection," "mortify," "put off/put on") flow out of what *is* —not what might be. Grace gives before it demands. Identity precedes activity. Union fuels obedience.

The Moral Logic of Grace

Paul never begins a new section without connecting it to what came before. The "If/Since ye then be risen" anchors the practical to the doctrinal. In chapter 2 he reminded us that we died with Christ to the rudiments of the world—the empty philosophies and traditions that hold men captive. Now he adds that we have also been raised with Christ. His resurrection life has become ours.

There is, in Paul's reasoning, a moral logic to grace. If we have died with Christ, the old life cannot continue. Since we have been raised with Christ, the new life

79

must begin. The believer is not merely improved; he is reborn. Therefore the commands of verses 1–11 are not rungs on a ladder to God; they are the footsteps of those whom God has already raised.

And that is Paul's bridge into the practical: Since you have been raised, seek the things above. Since your life is hidden with Christ, set your affection heavenward. Since Christ is your life, display Him—mortify what belongs to the grave, and put on what befits the new creation.

The Mind Set on Things Above

Paul directs our attention heavenward: "Seek those things which are above." The verb seek (Greek zēteite) is present active imperative—calling for continuous action. This is not a single upward glance, but a sustained pursuit. To seek is to live with a fixed aim—to orient the soul toward the throne of God where Christ is seated.

This command assumes that the believer's affections have been liberated from earthly captivity. Before regeneration, we were bound to the dust; now our hearts have been lifted toward heaven. The mind that once groped in the shadows of speculation is now enlightened by divine reality. To seek the things above is therefore to order one's whole life around that new center—to let the gravitational pull of heaven direct every orbit of thought and desire.

Paul adds a second imperative: "Set your affection on things above, not on things on the earth." The phrase literally means "keep thinking on," or "continually fix your mind upon." The term "affection" (*phroneite*) speaks not merely of emotion but of mindset—the settled disposition of one's thoughts, aims, and values. Christian affection is not sentimentality; it is sanctified reason. What we ponder, we pursue; what we prize, we practice.

Christ Enthroned, Not Merely Resting

Paul grounds this call in the position of Christ: "Where Christ sitteth on the right hand of God." The word "sitteth" does not merely indicate rest after labor—it denotes enthronement after victory. Christ's redemptive work on the cross is finished, but His priestly ministry continues. He is not idle in heaven; He is interceding, reigning, and preparing all things for the day of consummation.

At the Father's right hand, Christ holds the place of ultimate authority. From that seat, He governs His church and sustains His people. Every command that follows in Colossians 3 flows from that reality. The believer's life is to be lived under the rule of a risen, reigning Savior.

To set your affection on things above is therefore to live in ongoing fellowship with that ascended Lord—to think, choose, and act from the vantage point of His throne. The Christian mind, aligned with Christ's position, begins to see earthly events from eternal perspective. We no longer interpret life by what stands immediately before us, but by what lies beyond. Decisions are no longer driven by the urgency of the moment, but by the permanence of eternity. When we begin to think from heaven's horizon, our priorities change. The trial that once felt crushing now looks momentary against the weight of glory. The success that once seemed vital now fades beside the joy of pleasing Christ.

It is like viewing a landscape from a mountain height. Standing in the valley, all one sees are obstacles— walls of rock and the winding path ahead. But from above, the whole course is visible: the beginning, the end, and the purpose of every turn. So the believer, lifted with Christ, learns to see life from the summit of redemption. The trials that once consumed us now appear small beside His majesty. The pleasures that once enticed us lose their luster in His light.

Heavenly-Minded, Not World-Neglecting

Yet Paul's command is not an invitation to escapism. To be heaven-minded is not to withdraw from the responsibilities of earth, but to engage them with eternal purpose. The Christian's head is in heaven, but his feet remain firmly planted in the soil of daily obedience.

When heaven governs the heart, earth finds its rightful size. Duties become sacred; suffering becomes seed; even ordinary labor becomes worship when done unto Christ. We do not despise the temporal—we redeem it by using it for eternal ends.

C.S. Lewis captured this balance well: "If you read history, you will find that the Christians who did most for the present world were precisely those who thought most of the next." The same could be said of Paul. His heavenly vision made him the most practical of men. The more his eyes were fixed on Christ's glory, the more his hands were busy in Christ's service.

That is what Paul calls us to—a perspective anchored in the heavens but active on the earth. When our hearts beat in rhythm with the throne, our steps find their direction on the ground. To be risen with Christ is to live each day under the sunlight of eternity.

The Life Hidden with Christ

"For ye are dead, and your life is hid with Christ in God." (vs. 3)

Here Paul unveils one of the most profound mysteries of the Christian life. The believer's existence is now bound up in the life of Another. The world cannot see this life; even we, at times, can scarcely trace it. It is hidden—not because it is uncertain, but because it is secure. The word hid suggests not concealment for secrecy's sake, but safekeeping within the inviolable presence of God Himself. Our true life is locked away in the chambers of divine preservation—beyond the reach of decay, defeat, or the accusations of the enemy.

To be "hid with Christ in God" means that our identity is no longer anchored in what can be touched, measured, or taken. The believer stands in a double shelter: in Christ, and Christ in God. As Noah was sealed within the ark, so the redeemed are enclosed within the Savior, safe from every storm. Nothing— neither tribulation, nor distress, nor death itself—can break through to touch that hidden life. The surface of life may tremble, but its foundation is unmoved.

In union with Christ, we share both His death and His resurrection. The same divine power that raised Him now pulses within us. Death may touch the body, but it cannot reach the life that is hid in God. Every believer already lives in two worlds at once: visible in the realm of time, yet alive in the realm of eternity. The Christian's biography has two addresses—the temporal and the heavenly—and only one of them is permanent.

Paul adds a marvelous promise: "When Christ, who is our life, shall appear, then shall ye also appear with him in glory." Many read this as purely future—the revelation of Christ at His coming. That is indeed the consummation, but the truth also operates in the present. The word appear (*phanerōthē*) means to be manifested—to come into open view. It speaks on two levels at once. First, it points to the *Parousia*, that glorious moment when Christ Himself will be revealed in the clouds, no longer veiled in humility but radiant in majesty, and every eye shall see Him. But it also speaks of the manifestation of His life within us. The same power that will unveil Christ to the world is already at work unveiling Christ in the believer. What is now living hidden inside of us—Christ's own life— will one day blossom out in full splendor.

The life that is hidden is not lifeless; it simply awaits its unveiling. Every time Christ's character is displayed through His people—every act of love, every quiet word of forgiveness, every moment of patient endurance—His glory is already being manifested. These are the first rays of the sunrise that will one day fill the world with light.

This means that sanctification is not a slow climb toward something we do not yet possess—it is the uncovering of what is already ours in Christ. We often think of ourselves as sinners striving to become saints, but Paul's order is the reverse: we are saints learning not to act like sinners. The old man is not being rehabilitated; he is dead. The new man is not under construction; he has already been put on.

Sanctification, then, is not the process of becoming something different—it is the process of revealing who we truly are. The Spirit is steadily peeling away the remnants of the graveclothes so that the life of Christ within might be seen in full light. The Christian walk is the unveiling of a glory that has been hidden all along.

Putting to Death What Belongs to the Earth

Paul next moves from principle to practice:

> *"Mortify therefore your members which are upon the earth; fornication, uncleanness, inordinate affection, evil concupiscence, and covetousness, which is idolatry: for which things' sake the wrath of God cometh on the children of disobedience." (vv. 5-6)*

The word *mortify* means to put to death, to cut off what no longer belongs to the living. Paul's command is not the call of a harsh ascetic, but the call of a gardener who knows that life flourishes only when the dead wood is pruned away. Since we have been raised with Christ, the old life has no rightful place among the living. The Christian does not merely restrain sin; he removes its claim.

Paul lists five vices that thrive in the soil of the fallen heart—five weeds that choke the fruit of the Spirit. They move from outward action to inward motive:

- Fornication (*porneia*)—all sexual immorality, the misuse of God's good gift of intimacy.

- Uncleanness—the pollution that defiles even when unseen.

- Inordinate affection—passions that overstep the bounds of holiness.

- Evil concupiscence—desire itself turned toward what God forbids.

- Covetousness, which is idolatry—the craving to possess what only God can give, a worship of the created in place of the Creator.

Covetousness crowns the list because it exposes the root of them all: misplaced worship. Every sin begins as idolatry of self. When we crave satisfaction outside of Christ, we declare, in effect, that He is not enough. Thus, idolatry is not confined to altars and images; it thrives in ambitions, appetites, and comparisons.

Paul reminds his readers that the wrath of God comes upon such things—not the blind fury of a temperamental deity, but the settled opposition of divine holiness against all that destroys His creation. God's wrath is love in defense of righteousness. He will not permit what He loves to be ruined by what He hates.

Then comes the gentle reminder: "In the which ye also walked some time, when ye lived in them." The apostle never forgets the mercy that rescued him. He does not scold but shepherds. "You once lived this way," he says, "but not anymore." Grace does not merely pardon the sinner; it transforms the walk. The believer who remembers what he was will more readily extend compassion to those still bound by sin.

The call to mortify the old nature, then, is not a summons to self-loathing, but to self-reckoning—to agree with God about what has already died with Christ. We prune not to earn life but because we have it. Every act of repentance is a resurrection act, cutting away what belongs to the grave so that the life of Jesus may be seen in us.

Then comes a gentle reminder:

> *"In the which ye also walked some time, when ye lived in them." (v. 7)*

We were once no different. Every believer has a past tense. The ground of humility is the memory of mercy.

Putting Off and Putting On

"But now ye also put off all these; anger, wrath, malice, blasphemy, filthy communication out of your mouth. Lie not one to another, seeing that ye have put off the old man with his deeds; and have put on the new man, which is renewed in knowledge after the image of him that created him." (vv. 8-10)

If the first list of sins (vv. 5–7) deals with the lusts of the flesh, this second list deals with the temper of the heart. Having told us what to put to death, Paul now tells us what to put away—the habits and attitudes that no longer fit a soul clothed in Christ. The image changes from burial to wardrobe. The believer is not patching up the old garment of Adam, but exchanging it for the robe of the Second Adam.

"But now ye also put off all these." The verb implies a deliberate action—like removing a soiled coat and setting it aside once for all. Each word that follows describes a stain that once marked our old life:

- Anger—the smoldering heat of resentment that waits for a spark.

- Wrath—the eruption that follows, anger unrestrained.

- Malice—the lingering ill-will that plans another's hurt.

89

- Blasphemy—speech that defames, whether aimed at God or man.

- Filthy communication—corrupt, degrading talk that poisons what it touches.

Then Paul adds, "Lie not one to another." Falsehood destroys fellowship; truth binds it. The Church cannot be knit together in love (2:2) while it is frayed by deceit. Every lie is a return to the serpent's tongue— the first language of the old creation. But those who have been raised with Christ must speak the language of the new.

The reason for this moral wardrobe change is not self-improvement but identity:

> *"Seeing that ye have put off the old man with his deeds, and have put on the new man."*

The verbs are past actions with present effects. At conversion, God stripped off the old garment of sin and clothed us in Christ's righteousness. The old man —the self ruled by sin—was crucified with Christ. The new man is not an improved version of the old; he is a new creation entirely, "renewed in knowledge after the image of Him that created him." Redemption restores what Eden lost. The image of God, marred by sin, is being remade in the likeness of Christ.

This renewal is ongoing—"renewed" is present tense, a continuous transformation through the Word and the

Spirit. The more we know Christ, the more His likeness is reflected in us. As Romans 12:2 says, "Be ye transformed by the renewing of your mind." Discipleship is the daily wardrobe of grace—the conscious choice to live in the reality of who we already are.

And this new identity abolishes every wall of human distinction:

> "Where there is neither Greek nor Jew, circumcision nor uncircumcision, Barbarian, Scythian, bond nor free: but Christ is all, and in all."

The cross levels the ground beneath every foot. In the old world, these divisions defined worth and belonging. The Jew prided himself on law, the Greek on intellect, the Barbarian on strength, the Scythian on ferocity, the slave on obedience, and the free on privilege. But in Christ, all these badges dissolve. There are no second-class citizens in the kingdom of grace. Christ is all—our identity, our righteousness, our unity—and He is in all who believe.

The Church, then, is a community of the newly clothed—souls once tattered by sin now radiant in Christ's likeness. We do not wear these garments to impress the world; we wear them to display the One who dressed us. Our uniform is grace, and our calling is to live up to the name we bear.

The old distinctions collapse in the presence of Christ. Ethnic pride, social rank, cultural background—all are rendered meaningless. The church is not a society of likeness but a fellowship of life. Christ is not merely among us; He is within us. He is the unifying life of His people.

The world divides; Christ unites. The world classifies men by what they do; Christ identifies them by whom they belong to. If you are in Christ, then Christ is your identity. All else is secondary, temporary, and passing.

Summary

Paul moves in Colossians 3 from revelation to response—from the supremacy of Christ to the submission of His people. Those who have died and risen with Christ must now live as citizens of another realm.

He calls us to seek the things above, not by withdrawal from the world but by living under heaven's authority. Our life is hidden with Christ, and Christ Himself is our life. The believer's task is not self-improvement but self-expression—allowing the indwelling Christ to be displayed.

Because this new life is real, the remnants of the old must die. Sin cannot coexist with resurrection power. The Christian prunes his life, not to earn salvation, but to bear fruit worthy of it. Anger, impurity, deceit—all belong to the graveyard of the old man.

In their place stands the new man, renewed in knowledge after the image of the Creator. The gospel creates a new humanity that transcends race, class, and culture. The believer's wardrobe is Christ Himself —His righteousness, His character, His life.

Application

1. Live from a New Location. The believer's life is no longer rooted on earth but anchored in heaven. Our coordinates have changed. To "seek those things which are above" is to let eternity dictate today's priorities. Ask not, What will this gain me now? but, What will this glorify forever?

2.

3. A Christian whose gaze is fixed on heaven becomes the most faithful servant on earth. When our affections are set above, our actions become holy below.

4. Starve the Old Nature. To mortify the earthly nature is not to practice asceticism but to refuse nourishment to sin. Temptation thrives on attention; starve it, and it withers. We prune the branches that bear no fruit, cutting away attitudes and habits that steal the sap of grace. Every Christian must wield the pruning knife. God may

use hardship, disappointment, or loss as His blade, but the purpose is always fruitfulness. The gardener's cuts are mercy in disguise.

5. Wear the Garment of Grace. We do not clothe ourselves; Christ has clothed us. Our task is to live worthy of the uniform we wear. Imagine a soldier representing his nation or a student in the colors of his school—he carries an identity larger than himself. So it is with us: we wear the likeness of Christ. When the world looks at us, they should see His character—truth instead of deceit, kindness instead of malice, purity instead of passion. The robe of righteousness should fit naturally because it was tailored by grace.

6. Remember Who You Are. Identity is one of the great crises of our age. People define themselves by ancestry, preference, occupation, or ideology. Paul sweeps all of that aside. "Christ is all, and in all." Your worth is not found in your performance but in your position—in Him. You are not an old sinner trying to be holy; you are a holy one learning not to sin. Live from that reality. When Christ, who is your life, appears through you, His glory is revealed to a watching world.

Prayer

Father,

we thank You that in Your mercy You have hidden our lives with Christ in Yourself. Help us to set our hearts on things above and to live each day as those who are already risen. Teach us to put to death what belongs to the earth, to put away anger and deceit, and to wear the righteousness of Your Son with humility and joy.

With Your Spirit's renewing power, transform our minds, prune our hearts, and let Christ be all and in all within us.

We pray these things to Thee, Father, with the Spirit, in the name of Jesus Christ our Lord.

Amen.

Rooted

5

The Garments of Grace

"Put on therefore, as the elect of God, holy and beloved, bowels of mercies, kindness, humbleness of mind, meekness, longsuffering;

Forbearing one another, and forgiving one another, if any man have a quarrel against any: even as Christ forgave you, so also do ye.

And above all these things put on charity, which is the bond of perfectness.

And let the peace of God rule in your hearts, to the which also ye are called in one body; and be ye thankful.

Let the word of Christ dwell in you richly in all wisdom; teaching and admonishing one another in psalms and hymns and spiritual songs, singing with grace in your hearts to the Lord.

And whatsoever ye do in word or deed, do all in the name of the Lord Jesus, giving thanks to God and the Father by him."

(Colossians 3:12–17, KJV)

Clothed for a New Life

Paul never writes theology for the sake of abstraction. His letters move from creed to conduct, from truth to transformation. Having shown in the previous section that believers have "put off the old man" and been "clothed with the new," he now describes what this new life looks like when it takes form in daily character. If the first half of the chapter deals with the death of the old nature, this portion describes the adornment of the new—what it means to wear the garments of grace.

Every person who has come to Christ has undergone a profound change of identity. The old self, governed by sin and bound to the earth, has been put to death. The new man has been raised in righteousness, united with Christ, and fitted for glory. That transformation is invisible to the world until it is expressed through conduct. Grace must be worn to be seen. So Paul begins this section with the same imagery he used before: "Put on therefore." The verb evokes the deliberate act of dressing oneself. Having laid aside the rags of the old life, the believer now puts on the robe of Christ's own character.

The Identity of the Believer (v. 12a)

Paul roots every command in identity. Before he tells the Colossians what to do, he reminds them who they are: "the elect of God, holy and beloved." These three titles are the foundation of Christian conduct.

The Elect of God

To be called elect is not to boast in privilege but to rejoice in position. Paul is not introducing a philosophical doctrine of predestination; he is describing a spiritual location. Those who are in Christ are the elect of God. Our election is not an isolated choice of individuals apart from the cross—it is the privilege of all who have come to share in Christ's life.

In Him we are chosen. Outside of Him there is no election at all. God chose Christ as the Redeemer before the foundation of the world, and all who are joined to Him by faith share that chosen standing. Election, then, is not an exclusive club; it is the gracious inclusion of every believer who has been united with Christ through faith.

This understanding guards against pride and confusion alike. The glory belongs not to the chosen, but to the Chooser—not to those who occupy the position, but to the One who provided it. The hammer has no merit of its own; its usefulness comes only from the craftsman who holds it. So it is with believers. God has selected ordinary vessels to display His extraordinary mercy.

To be in Christ is to be part of God's redemptive purpose, the people through whom He makes His glory known. Election, in that sense, magnifies His grace rather than human worth. It is not a status to claim but a calling to live out. Because the Son of God died and rose again, all who are in Him share the dignity of His victory. The believer's worth, then, is not intrinsic but bestowed—derived entirely from the One in whom he abides.

Holy and Beloved

The second title—holy—means "set apart." Holiness is not an attitude of superiority or withdrawal from the world; it is the state of being reserved for God's purpose. The fine china in a cabinet is not better than the clay dishes used every day; it is simply set apart for a special occasion. In the same way, believers are not holier than others by nature, but they are set apart for the sacred purpose of displaying God's glory. They cannot spend their lives on common pursuits because they belong to an uncommon Master.

The third title—beloved—reminds us that all God's dealings are governed by love. Holiness without love would produce pride; election without love would foster fear. But love transforms them both into security and joy. God's love is not drawn out by anything lovely in us; it flows from His own nature. He loves because He **is** love. To be "beloved of God" means to rest in an affection that cannot be earned, diminished, or lost. The believer's identity, then, is secure: chosen by the Father, set apart by the Spirit, and loved through the Son.

The Virtues of the New Man (vv. 12b–14)

Having declared who we are, Paul describes what we are to wear. The wardrobe of grace consists of attitudes that reflect the character of Christ Himself. The new man is clothed, not in the garments of self-effort, but in the fabric of divine virtues woven by the Spirit.

A Heart of Mercy

"Put on therefore...bowels of mercies." The word Paul uses—σπλάγχνα (*splanchna*)—refers to the inward parts, the seat of deep emotion. In both Hebrew and Greek thought, the bowels represented the center of human feeling—the place where compassion stirs before it becomes action. What Paul describes here is not mere natural sympathy, but the sanctified affection of the new man. The believer who has been made new in Christ has also received new emotions—holy affections shaped by the Spirit.

When we recognize that our fellow believers are also beloved of our Beloved, our hearts begin to feel toward them as He does. We grieve when they suffer, rejoice when they are honored, and extend mercy when they stumble. This is not sentimental softness, but the compassionate nature of Christ expressing itself in His people. Mercy, therefore, is not a weakness to be suppressed but a divine tenderness to be cultivated. The new man feels deeply because Christ lives deeply within him.

The world is ruthless toward weakness. It celebrates competition and applauds revenge. But the follower of Christ is called to a different standard—to feel what others feel and to act on their behalf. Mercy recognizes that no one is beyond the reach of grace because no one stands lower than where grace once found us.

Christ Himself is the perfect model. Isaiah foretold that "a bruised reed shall he not break." He strengthened the fainthearted, comforted the broken, and restored the fallen. To wear His heart is to mirror His compassion—to look at the wounded world and choose not indifference but mercy.

Kindness

The next garment is kindness—a quality so simple that it is often overlooked, yet so rare that its absence darkens the world. Kindness is grace in motion. It is the active expression of mercy, the readiness to bless others without expectation of return.

In a culture marked by harshness and suspicion, kindness shines with quiet power. It is not weakness; it is strength under control. It chooses gentleness where the flesh would choose dominance. The believer who practices kindness reflects the tenderness of Christ, who invited the weary to come and rest.

Humility

Humility is not self-deprecation but self-forgetfulness. As C. S. Lewis observed, "Humility is not thinking less of yourself, but thinking of yourself less." It is the posture of one who knows that everything he has is received from God. Pride measures worth by comparison with others; humility measures worth by proximity to Christ. When one stands near the cross, boasting becomes impossible.

The humble believer does not compete for recognition, because he serves for the pleasure of his Master. He does not crave the first place, because he knows that Christ took the lowest. Humility frees the heart from the tyranny of self and enables it to serve in joy.

Meekness and Longsuffering

Meekness is gentleness combined with strength—a spirit that could retaliate but chooses restraint. It is not weakness; it is power submitted to love. The meek believer does not need to assert his rights because he has entrusted them to God. Longsuffering, or patience, is the endurance of love over time. It is the willingness to bear with others, to persevere in kindness even when provoked.

Both virtues require divine grace. They are not natural to the human heart. Yet they are the visible marks of one who walks in step with the Spirit. In the fellowship of believers, where personalities differ and offenses arise, meekness and patience keep the body whole.

Forbearance and Forgiveness

Paul continues, "forbearing one another, and forgiving one another." The verbs are present tense, indicating continual action. Forbearance is the grace of putting up with one another. It is the daily patience that makes community possible. No congregation is without friction. The church is not a gathering of perfect people, but of redeemed sinners learning to live as one body.

Forgiveness goes deeper. It releases the debt owed by another. The measure of our forgiveness, Paul says, is "even as Christ forgave you." To remember how much we have been forgiven is to lose all claim to vengeance. The cross stands as the perpetual reminder that grace cancels what justice would demand.

Charles Spurgeon observed, "If any man thinks ill of you, do not be angry with him; for you are worse than he thinks you to be." The believer who truly grasps his own sin will find it easier to extend mercy to others. Forgiveness is not a feeling; it is an act of faith, trusting God to heal what others have wounded.

Love: The Bond of Completion

Finally Paul crowns the list: "Above all these things put on charity, which is the bond of perfectness." Love is the clasp that holds every other virtue in place. Without love, compassion hardens into duty, humility turns to self-pity, and patience becomes mere tolerance. Love completes the wardrobe of grace because it is the nature of Christ Himself.

Love in Scripture is not sentiment but self-giving. It is the choice to place another's good above one's own comfort. It is the decision of the will to act for another's benefit, regardless of emotion. In human relationships, love is the most practical of all virtues— it covers the gaps where other graces falter. It forgives the unkind word, endures the misunderstanding, and restores the wounded bond.

To love is to live as Christ lived. When believers "put on love," they display to the world the beauty of the gospel itself, for "God is love." This love binds the church together as a seamless garment, woven of many threads but united in one pattern.

Ruled by Peace (v. 15)

"Let the peace of God rule in your hearts, to the which also ye are called in one body; and be ye thankful."

Peace is not merely the absence of conflict; it is the active presence of harmony produced by Christ. Before salvation, we were at war with God—alienated, hostile, and self-governed. Reconciliation through the cross has brought us peace with God. From that relationship flows the peace of God—the inner assurance that He reigns over every circumstance.

But Paul here speaks of a third dimension: peace within the body. The verb "rule" means "to act as an umpire." Peace is to make the call in every dispute. When believers disagree or frustrations arise, the deciding factor should be: what preserves peace in the body?

This peace does not compromise truth or holiness. It does not ignore sin for the sake of comfort. But where issues are nonessential, peace should prevail. In a world quick to divide, the church must display the reconciling grace of its Savior.

Paul adds, "and be ye thankful." Gratitude is the companion of peace. A thankful heart finds it difficult to quarrel. Discontent magnifies offenses; gratitude dissolves them. When believers focus on what God has given rather than what they lack, unity flourishes. A thankful spirit is the soil in which peace grows.

Filled with the Word (v. 16)

"Let the word of Christ dwell in you richly in all wisdom."

The phrase "the word of Christ" (ὁ λόγος τοῦ Χριστοῦ) carries a double meaning—both from and about Christ. Grammatically, it can be read either as a subjective genitive ("the word spoken by Christ") or as an objective genitive ("the word concerning Christ"). Paul likely intends both. The Word is **from** Christ, for He is the living Author of all Scripture; and it is **about** Christ, for He is the living Subject of all Scripture. From Genesis to Revelation, the divine narrative centers upon Him.

Thus, the Word of Christ is not merely a record of His teachings or a collection of sacred writings—it is Christ Himself communicating His life to His people. Every time the believer opens the Scriptures, the risen Lord speaks afresh through the written Word by the ministry of the Spirit. When that Word dwells richly within us, the mind becomes a sanctuary where His voice is heard, and the heart becomes His chosen dwelling place.

This echoes the Old Testament commands to meditate on the Word day and night (Joshua 1:8; Psalm 1:2). From the beginning, God's people were called not merely to read His Word, but to rehearse it continually—to let it occupy their minds in every moment of the day. Meditation in Scripture is not mystical detachment; it is focused reflection—truth turned over in the heart until it becomes part of who we are. Both Testaments use words that describe verbal engagement rather than silent introspection. The Hebrew word *hagah* means "to murmur" or "to speak softly," and the Greek *meletaō* (used in passages such as 1 Timothy 4:15) carries the sense of "to rehearse aloud," "to practice," or "to give sustained attention to." Biblical meditation is not the emptying of the mind but the filling of it with the Word until every thought begins to echo God's truth.

This practice is intensely practical. As we drive to work, we can repeat the Scripture we read that morning. As we do our chores, we can whisper a verse to ourselves, letting it sink into our hearts. As we walk through trial or joy, we can recall a promise until peace and gratitude rise again. Meditation is the art of carrying the Word with us—rolling it over in conversation, prayer, and thought—until it reshapes our perspective and becomes the filter through which we process the world.

When believers live this way, Scripture moves from the page to the bloodstream. It informs decisions, corrects attitudes, tempers emotions, and guards speech. The Word no longer visits occasionally; it abides continually. And when the Word dwells richly within us, it fills our minds with Christ's thoughts and our hearts with Christ's peace.

As the Word fills our minds and hearts through meditation, it naturally begins to overflow into our relationships. What we have rehearsed in solitude becomes what we share in fellowship. Paul expands the command: "teaching and admonishing one another in all wisdom." We are to teach ourselves first —letting Scripture instruct, correct, and train our own hearts—and then to instruct one another, not merely in the knowledge of the text but in its wisdom, the practical application of truth in the daily tests and trials of life.

Knowledge gathers facts; understanding sees how they connect; but wisdom learns to live them out. Wisdom is the Word embodied—the truth of Christ practiced in our choices, reactions, and relationships. As believers walk through difficulty or decision, they demonstrate how the Word works in real life. Their lived obedience becomes a testimony and a lesson to others.

This is how the church grows—not merely through sermons but through the mutual sharing of truth among its members. When believers speak Scripture to one another—in counsel, encouragement, prayer, or song—the Word becomes the language of the community. The fellowship of the saints becomes a living classroom where Christ Himself is the Teacher, and every conversation has the potential to build up the body in love and wisdom.

"Psalms and hymns and spiritual songs" were the worship vocabulary of the early church. They were not performance but participation. To sing "with grace in your hearts to the Lord" means to sing with gratitude, as those who have freely received grace and now give praise in return. Worship is not confined to melody; it is the overflow of grace into expression.

All in the Name of Christ (v. 17)

"And whatsoever ye do in word or deed, do all in the name of the Lord Jesus, giving thanks to God and the Father by him."

This verse gathers the whole passage into one grand principle. There is no division between sacred and secular in the Christian life. Every word and deed, every task and conversation, falls under the lordship of Christ. To act "in His name" means to act as His representative—to do all that we do as though He were doing it through us.

110

This transforms the ordinary into worship. The believer's workbench, classroom, or kitchen becomes a place of service as holy as any pulpit. Even the most repetitive or unseen task can be an act of devotion when done for the Lord.

Gratitude again crowns the command: "giving thanks to God and the Father by Him." Thanksgiving keeps the believer's life aligned with grace. It turns duty into delight, service into song. The one who lives in continual gratitude walks clothed in the garments of grace.

Summary

Paul paints the portrait of a life transformed by union with Christ. Those who are "the elect of God, holy and beloved" have been clothed in new garments—divine virtues that reflect their Savior's character. Mercy replaces hardness, kindness softens pride, humility bows before others, patience endures injury, forgiveness releases offense, and love binds all these graces together in perfect harmony. Peace rules the heart where Christ reigns; gratitude becomes the atmosphere in which believers live. The Word of Christ fills the mind and governs the tongue, turning every conversation, song, and action into an expression of worship. In Christ, the believer is no longer defined by the world but dressed in the righteousness and compassion of the Redeemer.

Application

The garments of grace are not achievements we sew together—they are gifts we receive and wear daily. Every moment invites a choice: will we clothe ourselves in the old patterns of self or in the new life of Christ?

To put on mercy is to let His compassion guide our responses. To put on kindness is to choose gentleness when irritation arises. To put on humility is to step out of the spotlight and let Christ be seen. To let the peace of God rule is to surrender control and trust His hand in every circumstance.

When Scripture dwells richly within us, it changes the way we think and the way we see people. Meditation turns truth into instinct; gratitude turns service into worship. Our homes, workplaces, and churches become places where Christ's character is on display. The world will not see Christ by our creeds alone, but by our conduct—by the grace we wear in ordinary life.

Prayer

Father,

Thank You for clothing me in the righteousness of Your Son. Teach me to wear His character with humility and joy. Let mercy be my reflex, kindness my tone, and love my constant thread.

When peace begins to slip from my heart, remind me that Christ still reigns there. When frustration or fear rise, anchor me again in gratitude.

Fill my mind with Your Word until it shapes how I think, speak, and respond. May every word and deed bring honor to Jesus, through whom I live and move and have my being.

In Christ's name I pray,

Amen.

Rooted

6

Serving the Lord Christ

Colossians 3:18–4:18

"Wives, submit yourselves unto your own husbands, as it is fit in the Lord.

Husbands, love your wives, and be not bitter against them.

Children, obey your parents in all things: for this is well pleasing unto the Lord.

Fathers, provoke not your children to anger, lest they be discouraged.

Servants, obey in all things your masters according to the flesh; not with eyeservice, as menpleasers; but in singleness of heart, fearing God:

And whatsoever ye do, do it heartily, as to the Lord, and not unto men;

Knowing that of the Lord ye shall receive the reward of the inheritance: for ye serve the Lord Christ.

But he that doeth wrong shall receive for the wrong which he hath done: and there is no respect of persons.

Masters, give unto your servants that which is just and equal; knowing that ye also have a Master in heaven." (Colossians 3:18–4:1, KJV)

"Continue in prayer, and watch in the same with thanksgiving;

Withal praying also for us, that God would open unto us a door of utterance, to speak the mystery of Christ, for which I am also in bonds:

That I may make it manifest, as I ought to speak.

Walk in wisdom toward them that are without, redeeming the time.

Let your speech be alway with grace, seasoned with salt, that ye may know how ye ought to answer every man." (Colossians 4:2–6, KJV)

The Lordship of Christ in Ordinary Places (3:18–4:1)

Paul's high Christology never floats above life; it lands squarely in kitchens and workshops, at supper tables and shop benches. The lordship of Christ is not an abstract doctrine for ivory towers or hymnals—it is the heartbeat of ordinary discipleship. The same Christ who reigns over thrones, dominions, and powers (1:16) also reigns over chores, conversations, and paychecks. Having exalted Him as Creator and Head (1:15–20) and having clothed the believer with the new man (3:1–17), Paul now shows how that supremacy shapes the most common arenas of human life. The gospel that reconciles heaven and earth must also reconcile husband and wife, parent and child, master and servant.

In the Roman world, these relationships were defined by hierarchy and control; the household (*oikos*) was a miniature empire where power flowed one direction—down. Paul's vision upends that structure. In Christ, authority becomes service, submission becomes worship, and work becomes ministry. Each role is reinterpreted through the lens of divine lordship. The wife's obedience is "as it is fit in the Lord" (v. 18); the husband's love mirrors Christ's self-giving; the child's obedience pleases the Lord; the father's restraint reflects the Father's gentleness; and even the bondservant's unseen labor is "unto the Lord, and not unto men." (v. 23)

Thus, the refrain beneath every command rings like a steady drumbeat: "For ye serve the Lord Christ." (v. 24) The Christian home is not governed by mere social order, but by worship. Every relationship becomes a place of devotion; every task, a liturgy. Paul refuses to separate theology from daily life because Christ Himself refuses to stay confined to the sanctuary. His lordship fills the home, the workplace, and the world— and wherever He reigns, sacred purpose transforms the ordinary into holy ground.

> **Greco-Roman Household Codes**
>
> *Cultural frameworks that regulated relationships within the home, assigning authority and obligation according to status and role. Paul engages this structure in Colossians by affirming order while radically reshaping it around Christ's lordship and mutual accountability.*

Wives and Husbands (3:18–19)

"Wives, submit yourselves unto your own husbands, as it is fit in the Lord." (v. 18) The word translated submit (*hypotassō*) comes from a military term meaning "to arrange under" or "to align oneself beneath for the sake of order." It describes not a loss of worth, but the willing arrangement of roles within a structure designed for harmony. In military use, it did not denote inferiority of rank in essence, but distinction of function for the sake of unity and purpose. Paul borrows this language not to impose hierarchy, but to illustrate order—a voluntary, Spirit-wrought disposition that recognizes God's design for the family.

Submission here is not servility or silence, but strength under guidance—a readiness to cooperate rather than compete. It flows from trust in Christ, not fear of man. The phrase "as it is fit in the Lord" both defines and limits the command. It means "as is proper," that is, as consistent with one's identity in Christ. It guards against abuse on one side and rebellion on the other: no authority may demand what Christ forbids, and no husband may claim what Christ withholds. In this light, submission becomes an act of worship, not weakness. It is the wife's way of honoring the order of creation while resting in the sufficiency of redemption.

In Christ's household, headship is never tyranny and submission is never servitude. Both husband and wife stand equal in value, dignity, and inheritance, yet distinct in calling. The wife's submission mirrors the church's glad obedience to Christ, just as the husband's love must mirror Christ's sacrificial care for

His bride. Together, they preach the gospel in the language of daily life.

"Husbands, love your wives, and be not bitter against them." (v. 19) The command to love translates the Greek verb *agapaō*, the word used throughout the New Testament for the self-giving, sacrificial love of God revealed in Christ. In Paul's world, household codes normally addressed men as masters—commanding their authority, not their affection. But the gospel overturns that pattern. *Agapē* does not dominate; it dignifies. It does not repress or reduce, but raises and redeems. It is love that stoops to serve, that lifts another into fullness rather than pressing them into submission.

This love is not driven by impulse or attraction, but by covenant. *Agapē* chooses for the other's good even when emotion wavers. It is the love that led Christ to the cross—not because His bride was worthy, but because His heart was steadfast. Such love leaves no room for bitterness, resentment, or harshness. The phrase "be not bitter against them" forbids the slow corrosion of spirit that turns authority into tyranny. A husband may win compliance through strength, but only love wins trust.

Paul's vision is radical: he calls husbands to mirror the very heart of Christ. As Christ's love sanctifies His church, so a husband's love is meant to nurture and elevate his wife—to help her flourish under grace, not wither under pressure. Headship in the Christian home is not a right to rule, but a responsibility to serve. Wherever *agapē* leads, pride dies and tenderness reigns. Thus, in the redeemed household, the husband's leadership is cruciform—shaped by the cross, sustained by humility, and crowned with joy.

Children and Fathers (3:20–21)

"Children, obey your parents in all things: for this is well pleasing unto the Lord. Fathers, provoke not your children to anger, lest they be discouraged." (vv. 20–21)

Paul turns next to the relationship between parents and children, and again his concern is order rooted in love. The verb obey (*hypakouō*) literally means "to listen under"—to hear attentively with a readiness to respond. It pictures a child who recognizes in parental instruction the voice of care and the wisdom of experience. The motive is not fear of punishment but the desire to please the Lord: "for this is well pleasing unto the Lord." The family, when ordered by grace, becomes a living parable of divine relationship—where the obedience of children mirrors the glad obedience of the believer to the heavenly Father.

But Paul immediately balances the command with a warning: "Fathers, provoke not your children to anger, lest they be discouraged." The word provoke (*erethizō*) means to irritate, exasperate, or embitter.

Paul knew that authority, if harsh or arbitrary, can crush the very hearts it's meant to shape. The ancient world often saw children as property or labor; the gospel sees them as persons—image bearers of God, entrusted to parents for nurture, not domination. The parallel in Ephesians 6:4 expands the thought: "Bring them up in the nurture and admonition of the Lord."

This verse dignifies both roles. The child's obedience honors God's design; the father's gentleness reflects God's heart. Parental discipline, when ruled by love, becomes discipleship—a training of both heart and habit. But when discipline turns into discouragement, it misrepresents the Father in heaven, who corrects His children always for their good, "that we might be partakers of His holiness" (Heb. 12:10).

In Christ, the home is transformed from a command post into a classroom of grace. Parents teach not by pressure, but by pattern—modeling faith, patience, and forgiveness. Children learn not just to submit to authority, but to trust the goodness behind it. Where Christ reigns, obedience and tenderness walk hand in hand, and the family becomes a reflection of the Father's household above.

Servants and Masters (3:22–4:1)

The gospel penetrates even the most entrenched social structures of the ancient world. Paul does not sanctify injustice, nor does he pretend that the structures of Rome are righteous. Instead, he inserts Christ into the very heart of each relationship. He transforms not the institution first but the individuals within it—reordering motives, purifying attitudes, and bringing all labor under a new Master.

"Servants, obey... not with eyeservice, as menpleasers; but in singleness of heart, fearing God." The new motive is worship: "Whatsoever ye do, do it heartily, as to the Lord, and not unto men." The most menial task becomes holy when offered to Christ. The believer's workplace is an altar. The command is radical not because it affirms the system but because it redefines service. Obedience is no longer a horizontal transaction but a vertical act of devotion. The smallest task, the most hidden labor, the daily grind done in obscurity—when performed unto Christ becomes sacred. The routine becomes liturgy; the servant becomes a priest whose common duties rise like incense before God.

Then Paul announces a truth so astonishing it must have sounded impossible in Roman ears: "Knowing that of the Lord ye shall receive the reward of the inheritance." Slaves in the ancient world possessed nothing. They could not inherit; they were inheritance. Yet Paul says that in Christ they receive the same eternal portion as the highest saint. The gospel gives what society withholds. Christ elevates the lowly, not by altering their station but by granting them a status the world cannot touch. The inheritance promised to sons and daughters of God outruns every inequity of earth.

Nor does Paul neglect justice. He adds, "He that doeth wrong shall receive for the wrong which he hath done: and there is no respect of persons." Final accountability belongs to God. Masters and servants alike will stand before the same Judge. No rank will shield the oppressor; no insignificance will silence the oppressed. God's court knows no partiality. He sees, He weighs, He repays. The gospel therefore comforts the mistreated and cautions the powerful. It announces that wrongs will not be forgotten, and that righteousness will have the last word.

Though Roman law offered several formal paths to manumission—through a magistrate's declaration, enrollment in the census, or a provision in a master's will—another practice was also well known throughout the wider Greco-Roman world: sacral manumission, the freeing of a slave through a temple. In this ritual, the master "sold" the slave to a god before witnesses or inscribed the act on stone. Legally, the freedman became the "property" of the deity. This did not create actual religious servitude; it was a legal fiction meant to protect the freedman from being enslaved again. No one dared seize the servant of Apollo or Zeus.

While this was not the only or even the primary Roman method of freeing slaves, the concept would have been familiar in the cultural imagination of Paul's readers. They understood the idea of a person being transferred to a new master—especially a divine one. Against this backdrop, Paul's words take on striking depth: "Ye serve the Lord Christ." Believers, whether slave or free, had been transferred to a new Master— not by temple ritual but by the blood of Christ; not by legal fiction but by spiritual reality.

This truth reshapes the entire household code. For the believing servant, obedience to an earthly master was no longer humiliation but consecration. Their labor passed through the lower authority and rose unto the higher One. They were not ultimately serving a household but a heavenly Lord. "Whatsoever ye do... do it heartily, as to the Lord, and not unto men." Their daily tasks—whether sweeping a floor or preparing a meal—became offerings placed on the altar of devotion. Their station did not define them; their Master did.

And because their true Master was Christ, they could serve with joy. Their circumstances were not chains but channels through which grace could flow. What others saw as servitude, the Christian slave understood as worship. Earthly masters could command tasks, but only Christ could command the heart. Freed from resentment, liberated from despair, the believing servant found dignity not in position but in belonging—belonging to Christ, the divine Master who rewards, remembers, and repays.

"Masters, give unto your servants that which is just and equal; knowing that ye also have a Master in heaven." As Paul turns to those who bear earthly authority, he does not soften the demand. The employer stands under employment; the master is himself mastered. Before he ever supervises another, he is supervised by Christ. The one who gives orders must take orders. Christian leadership is not license but stewardship, exercised under the gaze of the true Lord.

Paul commands masters to render "that which is just and equal." The two terms press different points. Just speaks to righteousness—doing what is right in God's sight, not merely what is required by custom or law. Equal speaks to fairness—recognizing the shared dignity of those under one's care, resisting partiality, and treating subordinates not as tools of production but as persons made in the image of God. Roman law granted masters nearly absolute power; the gospel binds that power with the cords of justice and equity. The Christian master must mirror the character of Christ, whose yoke is easy and whose burden is light.

This accountability is not abstract. Paul roots it in the most sobering truth: "knowing that ye also have a Master in heaven." There is no hierarchy before the throne that excuses cruelty, dishonesty, or neglect.

The highest earthly authority stands level with the lowest servant in the presence of Christ. The Christian master is called to remember that he will one day answer to the same Judge, under the same standard, with no advantage of rank. Authority is not a shield from scrutiny but a summons to greater responsibility.

Taken together, Paul's household code does not enthrone the powerful; it enthrones Christ. The point is not to cement social order but to transform it from within by locating every relationship beneath the lordship of Jesus. Domestic life, parental discipline, and daily labor are re-cast as worship. Ordinary roles become holy callings. Husbands love as Christ loves; wives submit as the Church submits; children obey in the Lord; fathers nurture rather than provoke; servants work as unto Christ; masters govern as those governed by Christ. Every corner of the household is illuminated by the presence of the true Master. When Jesus is Lord, hierarchy becomes humility, authority becomes service, and the entire fabric of life becomes an arena for obedience, devotion, and grace.

Summary

In this section, Paul brings the supremacy of Christ out of the heavens and into the home. The One who rules thrones and dominions also rules dinner tables and daily labor. By unfolding the household code,

Paul shows how the new man in Christ reshapes the most ordinary human relationships. Husbands and wives, parents and children, servants and masters—all find their roles reinterpreted through the lordship of Jesus. Submission becomes an act of worship; love becomes self-giving service; obedience becomes glad devotion; discipline becomes gentle nurture; labor becomes liturgy; and authority becomes accountable stewardship.

Paul does not bless the power structures of Rome, nor does he call believers to tear them down by force. Instead, he plants Christ at the center of each relationship so that transformation grows from the inside out. The refrain that binds every command together is simple and sweeping: "For ye serve the Lord Christ." The Christian home is no longer governed merely by custom or culture, but by a Person—the risen Lord whose presence turns ordinary duties into holy offerings. Under His reign, the household becomes a living demonstration of the new creation, where every role finds dignity, every task finds meaning, and every relationship becomes a theatre for the grace of God.

Application

Paul's vision for the Christian household confronts our modern assumptions as sharply as it confronted the ancient world. We are prone either to idolize personal autonomy or to misuse authority, but the gospel redirects both impulses by placing Christ at the center. Every believer, whatever his or her role, is called to live under the lordship of Jesus. This means wives submit not out of fear, but out of trust in Christ; husbands love not to maintain control, but to mirror Christ's sacrificial care; children obey not to avoid punishment, but because such obedience delights the Lord; and parents discipline not to dominate, but to nurture hearts toward God.

In our vocations, Paul's teaching is equally radical. We tend to divide life into sacred and secular, imagining that God receives our prayers but not our paperwork, our worship but not our work. But in Christ, "whatsoever ye do" is offered unto the Lord. Whether we sweep a floor, lead a team, prepare a meal, or serve a customer, every task becomes holy when done for Christ and in His strength. Conversely, those who exercise authority must remember they do so as servants of a greater Master. Supervisors, employers, leaders—whether in the workplace, church, or home—are called to treat those under their care with justice, fairness, and dignity, knowing that they, too, will give an account to the Lord.

Ultimately, this passage calls the believer to embrace the sacredness of the ordinary. Christ is not confined to church services or quiet devotions; He reigns in the rhythms of daily life. To follow Him is to bring His character into marriage, parenting, labor, and leadership. When we live this way, the world glimpses a household—and a people—who embody the beauty of the gospel in the smallest and most consistent acts of obedience. In serving others, we serve the Lord Christ.

Prayer

Father,

With the help of Your Spirit, we thank You for giving us Christ as our Lord, our Master, and our example. Shape our homes by His grace and bend our hearts to His will. Teach wives to submit with trust in You, and husbands to love with the tenderness of Christ. Guide children to obey with joy, and parents to nurture with patience and wisdom. In our labor, make our hands diligent and our motives pure. In our leadership, make us just, fair, and mindful that we also serve under Your authority. Let every task become worship, every relationship become ministry, and every moment become an opportunity to honor Your Son. Conform us to His likeness, that our homes and our lives may display His beauty. We pray these things to You, in the name of Jesus, with the Spirit.

Amen.

Rooted

7

The Watchful Life of Prayer

"Continue in prayer, and watch in the same with thanksgiving..." Colossians 4:2

The Christian life does not run on knowledge alone. It runs on breath.

Paul has taken us from the supremacy of Christ, to the indwelling of Christ, to the daily obedience demanded by Christ. Now he turns to the unseen power that fuels it all — prayer. Without prayer, doctrine hardens into theory. Without prayer, obedience becomes mechanical discipline. Without prayer, service slowly slides from dependence into self-reliance. Prayer is not the decoration of the Christian life; it is the oxygen of it.

This is not a casual suggestion. It is a call to persistence and depth. Paul uses the word προσευχῆ (*proseuchē*), not to describe a ritual or a formula, but a living, reverent conversation with God. This is prayer as communion, not performance — the soul consciously drawing near to the living God in humility, dependence, and trust. He then commands believers to προσκαρτερεῖτε (*proskartereite*) — to hold fast, to cling, to remain continually devoted. The word carries the sense of steadfast endurance, of refusing to loosen your grip even when the heart grows tired or the answer seems delayed. This is not the picture of a believer who prays only when convenient, or only when pain becomes unbearable. This is the portrait of a heart trained to remain before God — a soul that has learned that prayer is not a task to be completed, but a posture to be inhabited. Prayer is no longer something added to life; it becomes the air in which life is breathed.

A prayerless Christian is not merely undisciplined; he is unguarded. When prayer fades, discernment dulls, and the soul slowly loses its spiritual edge. Paul deepens the command by joining watchfulness to prayer, echoing the words of Christ in the garden: "Watch and pray, that ye enter not into temptation" (Matthew 26:41). Our Lord tied these two together because devotion without vigilance becomes softness, and vigilance without devotion becomes fear. God has designed them to function as one discipline — alertness rooted in dependence, awareness anchored in communion.

To watch in prayer is to remain spiritually awake, not restless, but ready. It is to resist the slow spiritual drowsiness that settles over the heart long before the conscience is alarmed. A believer who watches while he prays learns to recognize temptation while it is still forming and to sense danger while it still whispers. This alertness is not cultivated by suspicion, but by closeness. The nearer a soul lives to God, the faster it discerns what does not belong, and the more instinctive its resistance becomes.

The failure of the disciples in the Garden of Gethsemane stands as a sober warning to every generation of believers. Jesus did not ask them to preach, to fight, or to flee — He asked them to watch. Yet while the weight of redemption pressed upon His soul, those nearest to Him slept. This was not mere physical fatigue; it was spiritual dullness. Their eyes grew heavy before their hearts ever stirred. They loved Him, but they were unprepared to stand with Him in the hour of darkness.

When the test came, their drowsiness turned to panic, and their panic turned to flight. The sword flashed briefly in careless zeal, but it was no substitute for prayer. How often the same pattern repeats in our own lives: prayer neglected, vigilance abandoned, and then confusion when temptation arrives full-grown. The garden teaches us that it is not crisis that defeats us, but the unguarded moments long before the crisis ever comes.

Christ stood faithful where His disciples failed. He watched. He prayed. He submitted. While their spirits slept, His soul wrestled. While they sought comfort, He embraced the cup. And because He remained watchful, He was prepared to walk calmly toward the cross. The contrast is stark and merciful: sleeping disciples and a praying Savior. Our hope does not rest in our perfect vigilance, but in His. Yet His example remains our calling — not to sleep through danger, but to live in prayerful alertness before God.

If watchfulness keeps prayer alert, thanksgiving keeps it pure. Ungrateful prayer is not neutral — it is selfish at its core. When thanksgiving disappears, prayer does not become quiet; it becomes entitled. The heart begins to approach God as though He exists to serve rather than to be adored. Requests multiply, but reverence withers. Dependency fades, and expectation takes its place.

There is a subtle cruelty in this kind of prayer. It is not open rebellion — it is worse. It is familiarity without awe. It is the assumed right to blessing without the instinct to worship. It is living in the Father's house while behaving as though His presence is incidental. The soul becomes skilled at receiving and almost incapable of gratitude. When that posture settles in,

136

prayer ceases to be communion and becomes consumption.

Scripture warns us of hearts that live "without a sense of awe" — people who look spiritual, speak spiritual, and behave outwardly as they should, yet walk as though God were absent (Jude 17–19). This is not the spirit of mockery shouted in the streets; it is the quiet mockery of indifference. It is the contempt born, not of hatred, but of familiarity without gratitude. These were not pagans — they were among the assembly. They knew the language. They followed the patterns. But they lived as if God were not personally present.

Ungrateful prayer does the same thing. It asks for warmth but never acknowledges the fire. It seeks provision but rarely honors the Provider. It enjoys comfort and never considers the cost of grace. The soul becomes more concerned with personal ease than divine pleasure, more focused on satisfaction than surrender. Flesh grows bold when gratitude fades. Appetites expand. Sensory life dominates. Spiritual attentiveness shrivels.

Would we endure such treatment from our own children — obedience without affection, behavior without relationship, requests without thanks? How much more grievous is it when that spirit is carried into the presence of a holy God?

Thanksgiving rescues prayer from that slow corruption. It restores wonder. It returns the heart to humility. It reminds us that everything we have is mercy, everything we touch is grace, and everything awaiting us is promise — not because we deserve, but because He is good.

Paul makes prayer intensely personal in verse 3 when he turns the focus from general devotion to personal burden: "Withal praying also for us, that God would open unto us a door of utterance, to speak the mystery of Christ, for which I am also in bonds: That I may make it manifest, as I ought to speak." The great apostle does not request admiration, applause, or recognition — he asks for intercession. This is one of the quiet glories of true spiritual leadership: it does not posture strength, it confesses need. The man entrusted with unveiling the deep mysteries of Christ does not pretend self-sufficiency. He stands before ordinary believers and admits that his calling depends upon their prayers.

God has never advanced His kingdom through self-sufficient men. He advances it through praying people. This is why Paul's request is so revealing. He does not ask for comfort, nor relief, nor personal safety. He does not ask that chains be removed or circumstances softened. Instead, he asks for opportunity — that God would open a door for the Word. Though he sits behind iron doors, hearing the weight of chains and feeling the confinement of stone, he does not ask for prison doors to open. He asks for gospel doors to open.

This reveals the true priority of a surrendered heart. The self-preserving heart asks, "How do I get out?" The Christ-centered heart asks, "How do I get the Word in?" Paul does not view his imprisonment as interruption, but as assignment. He was not chained despite the gospel, but because of it. His bonds were not evidence of failure, but of faithfulness. He was content to remain confined, if only the mystery of Christ might be declared.

His final request uncovers the deeper burden of his soul: that he might make the message clear — "as I ought to speak." This is not the anxiety of a timid preacher, but the reverence of a faithful one. He does not ask for softer words, safer tone, or cultural approval. He asks for clarity. There is a way Christ ought to be spoken of — plainly, boldly, faithfully — without dilution or distortion. Paul felt the holy weight of that responsibility. Even an apostle trembled under the fear of misrepresenting his Lord. Even a seasoned servant felt the sobering burden of speaking heavenly truth with earthly lips.

This is the heartbeat of a true servant of God: not the craving to be heard, but the fear of speaking wrongly. Prayer is what fuels that kind of obedience. It is what keeps the tongue steady, the message pure, and the heart submitted. Without prayer, speech becomes careless. With prayer, speech becomes consecrated.

Summary

Colossians 4:2–4 reveals prayer as the living pulse of a faithful Christian life. Paul does not present prayer as religious ornamentation, but as spiritual respiration. To "continue in prayer" is to live in constant, reverent conversation with God — not as ceremony, but as communion. To "watch" in prayer is to stay spiritually awake, resisting the slow drift of dullness that leaves the soul vulnerable long before open sin appears.

Thanksgiving guards this sacred conversation from corruption. Without it, prayer turns inward and becomes entitled, demanding rather than dependent. Ungrateful prayer loses wonder, loses humility, and loses its sense of holy presence. A thankful heart, however, restores prayer to its rightful place — not as leverage over God, but as surrender before Him.

Paul then draws this truth into real ministry by making prayer personal. He asks the church to pray for him, not for comfort or escape, but for opportunity. Bound in chains, he does not ask for open prison doors but for open gospel doors. His burden is not safety, but faithfulness. His longing is not preservation of self, but clarity of speech.

This passage shows us that the strength of the church does not rest in confidence, talent, or independence, but in watchful, thankful, God-centered prayer. The work of God moves forward through humble people who know they cannot stand or speak without divine help.

Application

1. Prayer must become posture, not practice. Ask yourself whether prayer is something you visit or something you live within.

2. Watchfulness must be trained, not assumed. Consider where spiritual dullness may be settling quietly in your life.

3. Thanksgiving must be cultivated deliberately. Examine whether your prayers sound more like worship or more like expectation.

4. Pray for God's purposes, not just your comfort. Train your heart to ask for open doors for the Word, not merely easier circumstances.

5. Speak for Christ with reverence. Let your words grow out of prayer, not impulse. Ask God to help you speak as you ought, not as you wish.

Examine your heart:

- Do I pray to commune or to consume?

- Do I watch, or do I drift?

- Do I ask God for escape, or for obedience?

Let the Spirit retrain your heart so that prayer becomes breath, watchfulness becomes instinct, and thanksgiving becomes reflex.

Prayer

Father,

Thank You for inviting us into real, living conversation with You. Forgive us for the moments we have treated prayer as a task instead of a refuge. Teach us to remain with You, not only in crisis, but in every ordinary moment of life.

Keep our hearts awake. Guard us from spiritual drift and quiet forgetfulness. Train our souls to be watchful without fear and grateful without pretense. Where our prayers have become selfish or careless, gently restore wonder and humility within us.

Open doors for Your Word through our lives. Give us courage to speak clearly, wisdom to speak faithfully, and reverence to speak truthfully. Shape our words so they honor You, and shape our hearts so they belong fully to You.

We ask this in the name of Jesus,

Amen.

Rooted

8

Walk in Wisdom

In the previous passage, Paul called the church to persistent, watchful, thankful prayer and urged believers to pray that God would open doors for the Word (4:2–4). Prayer, however, does not end when the door opens. It trains the heart to recognize when opportunity appears and prepares the life to step through that opportunity wisely. What believers ask God to do in prayer must shape how they live when the answer arrives.

Seized Opportunities

Paul now turns from praying for open doors to walking wisely through them. A church devoted to prayer must also be a church attentive to opportunity—alert in conduct, deliberate in speech, and prepared to respond when outsiders are placed in its path. The movement from prayer to practice is not a shift in subject, but the natural progression of a life rooted in dependence on God.

"Walk in wisdom toward them that are without, redeeming the time." Colossians 4:5

Paul's language is deliberate. He speaks of walking because the Christian life is not merely professed; it is lived. Belief takes on shape through patterns, habits, and choices. Wisdom is not an abstract possession but a practiced way of life. To walk in wisdom is to move through the world attentively, thoughtfully, and intentionally, guided by the fear of the Lord rather than impulse or convenience.

Paul also names the audience: *"them that are without."* This phrase refers to those outside the fellowship of Christ—those who do not yet belong to Him or His body. Paul is not encouraging suspicion or withdrawal. He is reminding believers that the line between the church and the world is real, and that Christ Himself is that dividing line. The church does not exist apart from the world, but within it, and therefore believers must learn how to live distinctly without becoming distant.

To walk wisely toward outsiders means at least this: our lives must make sense in light of the gospel we profess. If we speak of Christ's lordship yet live as though money, comfort, or reputation rules us, the contradiction will not go unnoticed. If we claim to trust God while responding to hardship with the same panic, bitterness, or dishonesty as the world, our confession is quietly emptied of meaning. Wisdom considers how our actions, priorities, reactions, and habits either commend Christ or subtly deny Him.

This often shows itself in very ordinary places. It is seen in how a Christian handles frustration at work when things go wrong, how he speaks about others when they are not present, how she responds to inconvenience, criticism, or unfair treatment. Outsiders may never comment on our theology, but they notice whether our faith governs our temper, our integrity, and our decisions when obedience is costly. When a believer responds with patience instead of retaliation, honesty instead of shortcuts, humility instead of defensiveness, the gospel quietly gains credibility.

This is not a call to flawlessness, but to integrity. It is the refusal to live carelessly in front of those who are watching—not because we seek their approval, but because we serve a holy Lord whose name is already attached to our lives. When our walk aligns with our words, the gospel does not merely sound true; it appears credible.

Paul adds urgency to this call: "redeeming the time." The word he uses carries the idea of buying up an opportunity—seizing something valuable before it slips away. He is not warning believers merely about wasted minutes, but about wasted moments. Time here is not simply duration; it is opportunity. Doors open briefly. Conversations arise unexpectedly. Hearts soften in seasons of pain, curiosity, or crisis. Wisdom recognizes these moments and treats them as precious.

This often appears in unspectacular ways. A conversation lingers after a meeting has ended. A coworker speaks openly about fear, grief, or uncertainty. A neighbor asks a casual question that reveals deeper unrest. Such moments are easy to ignore or deflect in the name of busyness, comfort, or social ease. Yet they are often the very doors believers have prayed God would open. To redeem the time is to recognize those moments not as interruptions, but as invitations.

This does not require forcing conversations or delivering rehearsed speeches. It requires attentiveness. A redeemed moment may be as simple as listening when others would rush on, speaking a measured word of hope when silence would be easier, or offering prayer when the opportunity quietly presents itself. These moments rarely announce themselves as significant, yet they often carry eternal weight. Opportunity neglected is rarely recovered. Opportunity stewarded becomes obedience.

Christians are not called to drift through life inattentively. We are called to live awake. This does not deny the goodness of rest, but it does confront a culture—and a heart—prone to distraction and self-indulgence. A rooted life learns to ask not only, "What do I enjoy?" but, "What is God doing here?" To redeem the time is to recognize that God places His people among outsiders with purpose, and that opportunity neglected is opportunity lost.

Salted Speech

A wise walk will inevitably involve communication. When people walk together, they naturally speak to one another. Shared paths create shared conversation. It would be strange to journey side by side for miles in silence, and it is no less unnatural to imagine believers living among others without words ever accompanying their walk.

Scripture gives us a vivid picture of this in Christ Himself. On the road to Emmaus, the risen Lord walked alongside two discouraged disciples. Their steps were slow, their understanding was clouded, and their words were marked by confusion and disappointment. Jesus did not separate wisdom from speech. He listened, asked questions, and then answered their misguided remarks with patient, purposeful instruction, opening the Scriptures and addressing their hearts as they walked (Luke 24:13–27). His wisdom was not abstract; it was spoken, timely, and fitted to the moment.

Paul assumes the same rhythm here. As believers walk wisely among those who are outside—sharing the same terrain of daily life—conversation will follow. Our conduct prepares the way, and our speech gives voice to what our lives already proclaim. Wise walking does not replace words; it prepares them. And speech shaped by grace and truth is how wisdom is carried forward on the path we share with others. "Let your speech be alway with grace, seasoned with salt…" Colossians 4:6

Paul does not allow exceptions. Christian speech is to be always marked by grace. Grace does not mean flattery or softness; it means speech shaped by Christ Himself—truthful, patient, restrained, and aimed at the good of the hearer. Gracious speech does not seek to win arguments or assert superiority. It seeks to give— to give clarity, correction, encouragement, warning, or hope as needed.

Scripture closely links grace with the idea of gift, and Paul's instruction here draws from that shared language. The word translated grace is χάρις (charis). From the same root come χάρισμα (charisma), meaning gift, and εὐχαριστία (eucharistia), meaning thanksgiving. Grace is something freely given. A gift is the concrete expression of that grace. Thanksgiving is the fitting response to receiving it. Paul's point is that our speech should participate in that same gracious movement—given, not seized; offered, not imposed.

Words shaped by *charis* are therefore not weapons used to wound or dominate, but gifts offered deliberately and responsibly for the good of the hearer. This does not forbid hard truth—Scripture never avoids truth—but it does forbid careless truth. There is a way to speak accurately and still dishonor the Lord if our words lack grace. When speech ceases to function as a gift, it no longer reflects the gospel of grace it claims to proclaim.

When Paul speaks of speech "seasoned with salt," he is drawing on an image his readers would have immediately understood. In the ancient world, salt was not primarily a table seasoning; it was a preservative. Without refrigeration, meat and fish were packed in salt to prevent decay. Wine was salted to keep it from spoiling once opened. Salt did not make food temporary; it made it durable. What was salted was considered worth keeping.

Salt was also costly and valuable in the Roman world. It was a traded commodity, sometimes even offered as a soldier's compensation (thus the word *salary*), a necessary resource, and a symbol of worth. To salt something was to treat it as significant, not disposable. Paul's picture, then, is not of casual speech sprinkled lightly with charm, but of words prepared and preserved—what we might call *pickled speech*. Speech that has been brined, not rushed; speech intended to last, not merely to pass the moment.

This is Paul's point: Christian words should carry weight and durability. They should not rot into carelessness, nor evaporate into meaninglessness. Words shaped by grace and preserved with truth are worth holding onto. They are meant to be remembered, carried, and returned to in the heart long after the conversation has ended.

Salt also carried a cleansing function in the ancient world. It was used to clean wounds, to draw out corruption, and to prevent infection from spreading. The process was often painful, but it was purposeful. Salt stung because it healed. It did not create the wound, but it confronted what threatened to fester beneath the surface.

In the same way, speech seasoned with salt is not always comfortable, but it is always restorative. Paul is not calling believers to avoid difficult words, but to speak them in a way that cleans rather than corrupts. Salted speech addresses what is harmful without becoming harmful itself. It tells the truth without spreading decay, and it confronts sin without delighting in injury. When words are shaped by grace and preserved with truth, even correction becomes medicinal rather than destructive.

Salt also guards us from misunderstanding grace. Paul does not say "sweetened with honey." Grace does not dilute truth or soften it into something unrecognizable. Salt preserves; it does not erase. Speech that is both gracious and salted is speech that remains kind without becoming vague, and clear without becoming cruel.

Such speech takes time. Prepared words do not rush. They are considered before they are released. In a world addicted to noise and speed, silence itself can be an act of wisdom. I once knew a man who was a remarkably slow talker. When you asked him a question, he would pause—long enough to make you wonder whether he had heard, or whether he was finished altogether. Yet when he finally spoke, his words were always worth hearing. He had taken the time to prepare them. He did not waste speech, and because of that, he rarely wasted words.

Paul is calling believers to that same discipline. Rash speech often reveals pride—the assumption that the first thought deserves to be spoken. Measured speech reflects humility—the recognition that words carry weight and consequence. A rooted Christian learns that words, once spoken, cannot be retrieved, and therefore deserve patience and care. Speech seasoned with salt is not hurried; it is deliberate, responsible, and worthy of being remembered.

Paul concludes with the purpose of all this wisdom:

> *"that ye may know how ye ought to answer every man." Colossians 4:6*

The Christian life is not meant to be mute. Paul assumes that questions will be asked, objections raised, and conversations begun. He does not say believers must have an answer for everything, but that they should know how to answer—rightly, fittingly, and responsibly. That kind of readiness does not happen accidentally. It requires preparation long before the moment of response arrives.

Prepared speech is formed in quiet places. It grows out of time spent in Scripture, where the mind is shaped by truth rather than opinion. It is refined through personal meditation, where truth is pressed into the heart and tested against real life. It is sharpened through godly conversation, where believers learn to speak carefully, listen humbly, and think clearly alongside one another. Wisdom is not merely knowing what is true; it is knowing what is appropriate for the person before you. And that discernment is cultivated, not improvised.

Paul adds a final, important detail: "every man." The gospel does not come to people as a script delivered identically each time. Different hearts require different approaches. Some need gentle instruction. Some need firm correction. Some need patience. Some need clarity. Some need silence before speech. To answer each one well requires nearness to Christ, whose words were always true and always fitting.

This passage quietly reminds us that effective witness flows from communion with God. Watchful prayer produces wise walking. Wise walking gives rise to gracious speech. Gracious, salted speech prepares the way for faithful answers. A life rooted in Christ becomes a life ready for others.

Summary

Colossians 4:5–6 calls believers to a public life shaped by wisdom, purpose, and grace. Paul commands the church to walk wisely toward outsiders, living with discernment and integrity before a watching world. This wisdom is not isolation, but intentional presence—lives that quietly affirm the truth of the gospel they confess.

Paul then urges believers to redeem the time, treating opportunities as precious and fleeting. Life is not to be drifted through inattentively, but stewarded faithfully, especially when God opens doors for truth.

Christian speech must always be marked by grace and seasoned with salt—prepared, preserved, and purposeful. Words are not to be careless or destructive, but considered gifts offered for the good of others. Grace guards the heart; salt guards the truth.

Finally, Paul calls believers to readiness—to know how they ought to answer each person wisely and fittingly. A rooted life is not only stable and obedient; it is attentive, thoughtful, and prepared to speak Christ faithfully in real moments with real people.

Application

- **Walk intentionally before unbelievers.** Ask whether your daily life reflects wisdom or merely blends in.

- **Treat opportunities as sacred.** Pray for eyes to recognize moments God opens and courage to step into them.

- **Commit to gracious speech as a rule, not a reaction.** Decide ahead of time that your words will serve rather than wound.

- **Slow down your tongue.** Prepare your words before you speak them. Silence is often wiser than haste.

- **Answer people, not just questions.** Learn to respond thoughtfully to the soul before you, not merely the issue presented.

Rooted

Examine your heart:

- Do I walk wisely, or do I drift?

- Do I redeem opportunities, or overlook them?

- Are my words gifts, or weapons?

- Do I speak from impulse, or from prayer?

Let Christ train your steps and govern your tongue, so that your life and words together bear faithful witness to Him.

Prayer

Father,

You have placed us among those who do not yet know You, not by accident, but by Your wise design. Teach us to walk in wisdom, so that our lives do not contradict the Christ we confess.

Help us redeem the time You give. Open our eyes to opportunities for truth and love, and guard us from careless drift and wasted moments.

Set a watch over our mouths. Fill our speech with grace and preserve it with truth. Teach us to slow down, to consider, and to speak only what honors You and serves others.

Give us wisdom to answer each person as we ought, with clarity, humility, and faithfulness. Shape our lives so that Christ is seen, and our words so that Christ is heard.

We ask this in the name of Jesus,

Amen.

9

Rooted Lives, Shared Work

Paul closes his letter to the Colossians not with a final argument, but with names. After unfolding the supremacy of Christ, the sufficiency of Christ, and the transforming power of Christ in daily life, he ends by pointing to people. This is not an afterthought. It is a theological conclusion. Christianity is not an abstract system of ideas; it is a living faith that produces real relationships, shared labor, and visible community.

The gospel always moves from truth to people. Doctrine does not remain suspended in theory; it takes on flesh in ordinary men and women whose lives are bound together in Christ. Paul's greetings remind us that a life rooted in Christ is never lived alone.

All my state shall Tychicus declare unto you, who is a beloved brother, and a faithful minister and fellowservant in the Lord:

Whom I have sent unto you for the same purpose, that he might know your estate, and comfort your hearts;

With Onesimus, a faithful and beloved brother, who is one of you. They shall make known unto you all things which are done here.

Aristarchus my fellowprisoner saluteth you, and Marcus, sister's son to Barnabas, (touching whom ye received commandments: if he come unto you, receive him;)

And Jesus, which is called Justus, who are of the circumcision. These only are my fellowworkers unto the kingdom of God, which have been a comfort unto me.

Epaphras, who is one of you, a servant of Christ, saluteth you, always labouring fervently for you in prayers, that ye may stand perfect and complete in all the will of God.

For I bear him record, that he hath a great zeal for you, and them that are in Laodicea, and them in Hierapolis.

Luke, the beloved physician, and Demas, greet you.

Salute the brethren which are in Laodicea, and Nymphas, and the church which is in his house.

And when this epistle is read among you, cause that it be read also in the church of the Laodiceans; and that ye likewise read the epistle from Laodicea.

And say to Archippus, Take heed to the ministry which thou hast received in the Lord, that thou fulfil it.

The salutation by the hand of me Paul. Remember my bonds. Grace be with you. Amen. Colossians 4:7-18

The Gospel Creates Partners, Not Isolated Believers

Throughout this closing section, Paul repeatedly uses relational language: brother, fellow servant, fellow prisoner, faithful minister. These are not honorary titles. They describe shared labor under a shared Lord. Paul does not present himself as a solitary apostle surrounded by assistants. He presents a network of co-laborers—men whose lives and callings have been woven together by the gospel.

Tychicus is sent as a faithful messenger, entrusted to carry Paul's words and encourage the church. Onesimus is named as a "faithful and beloved brother," no longer defined by his past but by his place in Christ. Paul does not introduce him as a former runaway slave, but as a brother—because the gospel redefines identity before it recounts history.

This alone says much about what it means to be rooted. A Christ-centered faith does not cling to former labels. It recognizes what grace has done and treats believers accordingly. The church is not a museum of reputations; it is a community of renewed people.

Grace Redeems Failure and Restores Usefulness

Paul names Mark and notes that the Colossians have received instructions concerning him. This brief reference carries a quiet but powerful testimony. Mark had once abandoned the work and caused sharp disagreement between Paul and Barnabas. Yet here he stands restored, useful, and commended.

Paul does not rehearse the failure. He does not explain the reconciliation. He simply includes Mark as a fellow worker. That silence is itself instructive. Grace does not endlessly reopen old wounds. When repentance and restoration have done their work, grace moves forward.

A rooted life is not measured by an unbroken record, but by a redeemed one. The gospel does not eliminate failure; it transforms what failure means. Christ does not merely forgive; He restores to service.

Faithful Service Often Happens Quietly

Luke is named without elaboration, though history tells us much about him. Paul does not point to his writings or his skill. He simply includes him. Faithfulness does not require explanation. In a list of greetings, Luke stands as a reminder that much of God's work is done quietly, steadily, and without recognition.

The same is true of others Paul names. Aristarchus, Justus, Epaphras—each is described briefly, but meaningfully. Epaphras, in particular, is commended for his labor in prayer. His work is unseen, yet Paul presents it as strenuous and vital. The church is strengthened not only by preaching and teaching, but by faithful intercession that never appears on a stage.

Rooted lives do not all look the same. Some carry messages. Some pray. Some teach. Some serve in the background. Christ uses them all.

The Church Is Bound Together Across Distance

Paul's greetings stretch across geography. Some are with him; others belong to the Colossian assembly or nearby churches. Messages are exchanged. Letters are shared. Greetings are passed along. The picture is of a church not confined to one place, but united by one Lord.

Paul even instructs that his letter be read in Laodicea, and that the Colossians read the letter from there. The Word of Christ is not meant to remain local. Truth is to be shared, circulated, and received together. A rooted church does not hoard instruction; it participates in the wider body of Christ.

Paul's mention of Archippus carries a gentle exhortation: "Take heed to the ministry which thou hast received in the Lord, that thou fulfil it." This is not rebuke, but reminder. Calling received must be calling completed. Faithfulness is not measured by beginning well, but by finishing well.

Paul Ends Where He Began: With Grace

Paul closes the letter with a personal note, written in his own hand: "Remember my bonds. Grace be with you." The chains are not hidden. The cost is not denied. Paul does not romanticize suffering, but

164

neither does he allow it to dominate the letter's final word.

The final word is grace.

Grace that called him.

Grace that sustained him.

Grace that bound these believers together.

Grace that will continue to work long after the letter is read.

Colossians begins with Christ supreme over all things. It ends with grace resting upon His people. Between those two truths stands the Christian life—rooted in Christ, expressed in obedience, and shared among ordinary believers bound together by extraordinary grace.

Summary

Colossians ends not with abstract theology, but with real people whose lives have been shaped by Christ. Paul's greetings reveal that the gospel creates partnership, restores the fallen, values quiet faithfulness, and binds believers together across distance and difference.

These names testify that Christ's work is communal. No one carries the gospel alone. Different gifts, different roles, and different histories are gathered into one shared labor under one Lord. Failure is redeemed, service is restored, and faithfulness— whether visible or hidden—is honored.

Paul's final handwritten words remind us that grace, not circumstance, has the final say. The same grace that sustained him in chains sustains the church in every generation.

Application

- **Remember that faith is personal, but never private.** Rooted faith expresses itself in shared life and shared work.

- **Resist the temptation to measure usefulness by prominence.** God values faithfulness that is quiet and unseen.

- **Do not define others—or yourself—by past failure.** Grace restores and reuses what repentance has healed.

- **Finish the work God has given you.** Calling received is calling to be fulfilled.

- **Let grace be the final word in your life, just as it is the final word of this letter.**

Examine your heart:

- Am I rooted in Christ alone, or in my role?

- Do I value the unseen work of others?

- Am I walking forward in grace, or lingering in old labels?

- Am I committed to finishing what God has entrusted to me?

Prayer

Father,

Thank You for the grace that not only saves, but binds Your people together. Thank You for the quiet faithfulness of servants whose work You see even when others do not.

Teach us to live rooted lives—faithful, humble, and shared with others. Help us honor the work You give, restore what grace has redeemed, and finish our calling with endurance.

May Your grace rest upon us, shape our community, and carry Your work forward through ordinary lives surrendered to an extraordinary Christ.

We ask this in the name of Jesus,

Amen.

Appendix A: Christ and the Fullness of God

F ew concepts in Colossians are as central—or as easily misunderstood—as Paul's insistence that all the fullness of God dwells in Christ. This claim stands at the heart of Paul's argument against false teaching and at the foundation of the believer's confidence in Christ. To understand what Paul means by "fullness," we must consider both the term itself and the way Paul applies it to the person of Jesus Christ.

The Meaning of "Fullness"

The word Paul uses is πλήρωμα (*plērōma*), a term that refers to fullness, completeness, or that which fills something to its intended capacity. In everyday usage, it could describe a ship fully loaded, a container filled to the brim, or a measure brought to completion. Paul takes this common idea and applies it with extraordinary theological weight.

In Colossians, *plērōma* does not refer to a collection of divine attributes distributed among spiritual beings, nor to a spiritual reservoir that believers must access through religious practices or mystical experiences. Instead, Paul insists that fullness resides wholly and permanently in Christ Himself.

"For it pleased the Father that in Him should all fulness dwell" (Col. 1:19).

"For in Him dwelleth all the fulness of the Godhead bodily" (Col. 2:9).

Paul's language is deliberate. He does not say that fullness visits Christ, flows through Christ, or is mediated by Christ. He says it dwells in Him. The word carries the sense of settled residence. Fullness is not borrowed; it belongs.

Some later Gnostic systems would use the word *plērōma* to describe a hierarchy of divine emanations or spiritual intermediaries through which fullness was distributed in stages. While these systems reached their mature form after the time of Paul, Colossians already confronts the instinct behind them—the belief that divine fullness must be accessed indirectly, supplemented through spiritual ascent, or completed beyond Christ. Paul's response is not to refine such a concept, but to collapse it entirely by declaring that all fullness dwells, without remainder, in Christ Himself.

Fullness and the Nature of Christ

When Paul speaks of the fullness of the Godhead dwelling bodily in Christ, he is making a clear and uncompromising Christological claim. Jesus Christ is not partially divine, nor a lesser intermediary between

God and humanity. He is fully and truly God, incarnate in human flesh.

This matters because the false teachers troubling the Colossian church were not denying Christ outright. They were redefining Him. They treated Christ as essential but incomplete—one step in a larger spiritual system that required supplementation. Paul responds by closing every possible gap. If all the fullness of God dwells in Christ, then nothing of God lies outside of Him, and nothing can be added to Him.

To seek fullness elsewhere is not advancement; it is departure.

Fullness and the Believer

Paul does not stop with Christ's fullness. He presses the implication directly into the believer's life:

"And ye are complete in Him" (Col. 2:10).

The word translated "complete" is drawn from the same root as *plērōma*. Paul is not saying that believers possess divine fullness in themselves. He is saying that believers lack nothing because they are united to the One who is full. Fullness does not originate in the Christian; it is shared through union with Christ.

This distinction guards against two opposite errors. On the one hand, it protects against spiritual insecurity—the fear that something essential is missing. On the other hand, it guards against spiritual pride—the belief that fullness resides in the believer apart from Christ. Paul allows neither. Christ is full. Believers are complete in Him.

Fullness Versus False Fullness

The false teachers promised fullness through observance, experience, and insight. Paul exposes those promises as hollow. Practices that appear wise, severe, or spiritual may impress the flesh, but they cannot fill the soul. Anything that claims to complete what Christ has already completed ultimately competes with Him.

Paul's doctrine of fullness is therefore deeply pastoral. It is meant to settle the restless heart. It calls believers away from endless striving and back to confident dependence. Growth in Christ does not mean acquiring what He lacks, but increasingly living out what He has already supplied.

The Comfort of Fullness

For the believer, Christ's fullness is not an abstract doctrine but a stabilizing truth. It means forgiveness is complete, reconciliation is secure, authority is sufficient, and hope is certain. No spiritual deficit remains to be corrected by human effort or religious addition.

Christ does not merely point us toward fullness.

He does not guard fullness for later access.

He is the fullness of God given to us. To be rooted in Christ is to be rooted in fullness itself.

Summary

Paul's use of *plērōma* in Colossians affirms that all the fullness of God dwells permanently in Jesus Christ. This fullness is not distributed, supplemented, or accessed elsewhere. Because believers are united to Christ, they are complete in Him—not by possession, but by participation.

The doctrine of fullness anchors the believer's confidence, guards against false spirituality, and calls the church to rest in Christ rather than strive beyond Him. Nothing is lacking where Christ is present.

Rooted

Appendix B: Assurance, Perseverance, and Remaining in Christ

The letter to the Colossians contains some of Scripture's strongest affirmations of the believer's security in Christ. At the same time, it includes earnest calls to continue, remain, and walk faithfully in Him. For some readers, these themes can appear to pull in opposite directions—raising questions about assurance, perseverance, and the nature of saving faith. This appendix seeks to clarify how these ideas function together within Paul's teaching.

Assurance Rooted in Christ, Not Performance

Paul grounds the believer's assurance firmly and repeatedly in the finished work of Christ. Believers are described as reconciled, forgiven, and transferred into the kingdom of God's dear Son. These are not provisional realities, nor are they earned through continued effort. They are gifts of grace, received by faith.

Assurance, therefore, does not arise from self-examination alone, nor from the consistency of one's obedience. It rests in the objective reality of what Christ has accomplished. The believer's confidence is not found in the strength of their grip on Christ, but in the faithfulness of Christ's hold on them.

This guards the Christian from despair. Weakness, struggle, and even failure do not nullify the work of Christ. Assurance looks outward before it looks inward.

Perseverance as the Evidence of Life

While assurance is rooted in Christ's work, perseverance is the fruit of that work. Paul speaks plainly of continuing in the faith, remaining grounded, and not being moved away from the hope of the gospel. These exhortations do not imply that salvation is earned through endurance, but that genuine faith endures because it is alive.

Perseverance, in Scripture, is not a heroic achievement of the will. It is the steady, often imperfect continuation of faith under grace. Where life exists, growth and persistence follow—not flawlessly, but truly. A faith that utterly abandons Christ demonstrates not lost salvation, but the absence of saving faith to begin with.

This distinction matters. Perseverance does not create assurance; it confirms it. And it does so quietly, over time, rather than dramatically in moments of crisis.

Jesus' parable of the sower illustrates this distinction clearly. In the parable, several kinds of soil receive the seed, and some show immediate response. Yet only the seed that takes root and endures produces fruit. The issue is not initial enthusiasm, but lasting life. Where life is present, growth follows in time; where it is absent, collapse eventually reveals what was always true. Perseverance, then, does not prove the worthiness of the soil—it reveals its nature.

Remaining in Christ

Paul's language of "remaining" or "continuing" in Christ describes a living relationship, not a contractual arrangement. To remain in Christ is to abide where life is found—to continue trusting, depending, and drawing nourishment from Him.

This remaining is not passive. It involves resisting teachings that would pull the believer away from Christ's sufficiency, and refusing patterns of life that contradict union with Him. Yet it is not sustained by fear. It is sustained by attachment.

The image of rootedness is helpful here. Roots do not cling anxiously; they grow naturally where nourishment is present. In the same way, believers remain in Christ not by constant self-monitoring, but by continued reliance on Him.

Warnings as Means, Not Threats

The warnings found in Colossians—and throughout the New Testament—serve a vital purpose. They are not threats meant to destabilize assurance, but means God uses to preserve His people. They awaken the conscience, sharpen discernment, and call believers back to what is true when drift begins.

Such warnings assume a real danger, but they also assume a faithful Shepherd. God does not warn His children in order to abandon them, but to keep them. The call to continue is itself an expression of grace.

Holding the Tension Faithfully

Scripture does not ask believers to resolve every tension between assurance and perseverance into a single formula. It calls them to trust Christ fully and to follow Him faithfully. Where Christ is trusted, assurance grows. Where Christ is followed, perseverance appears.

The believer's hope rests not in perfect consistency, but in a perfect Savior. Christ is sufficient to save, sufficient to keep, and sufficient to bring His people safely home.

To remain in Christ, then, is not to live in fear of falling away, but to live confidently where life is found— rooted, established, and growing in Him.

Summary

Assurance rests in Christ's finished work, not in human endurance. Perseverance is the evidence of living faith, not the cause of salvation. Remaining in Christ describes an ongoing relationship sustained by grace, nourished by truth, and preserved by God Himself.

Together, these truths protect believers from both false confidence and unnecessary fear, calling them instead to steady trust in a Savior who is faithful to complete what He has begun.

Rooted

About the Author

James Burke is the senior pastor of Grace Community Church in Marinette, Wisconsin. With a passion for preaching God's Word and shepherding God's people, he has spent decades helping believers grow in faith and guiding churches toward gospel-centered health. His ministry is marked by a commitment to Scripture, a love for Christ's church, and a desire to see lives transformed by the power of the cross. When he isn't preaching or writing, James enjoys time with his wife Roxanne, meaningful conversations over coffee, and the beauty of life along the shores of Lake Michigan.

Rooted

www.ingramcontent.com/pod-product-compliance
Lightning Source LLC
Chambersburg PA
CBHW060421130626
46555CB00005B/2159